A Rulebook for Arguments

Anthony Weston

A Rulebook for Arguments

Third Edition

Hackett Publishing Company
Indianapolis/Cambridge

For further information, please address:

Hackett Publishing Company, Inc.
P.O. Box 44937
Indianapolis, IN 46244-0937

www.hackettpublishing.com

Cover and interior design by Abigail Coyle
Cover photograph: www.comstock.com

Library of Congress Cataloging-in-Publication Data

Weston, Anthony, 1954–
   A rulebook for arguments / Anthony Weston.—3rd ed.
      p. cm.
   Includes bibliographical references.
   ISBN 0-87220-553-3 (cloth)—ISBN 0-87220-552-5 (paper)
   1. Reasoning. 2. Logic. 3. English language—Rhetoric. I. Title.

BC177.W47 2000
168—dc21   00-058121

ISBN-13: 978-0-87220-553-6 (cloth)
ISBN-13: 978-0-87220-552-9 (pbk.)

Contents

Preface

This book is a brief introduction to the art of writing and assessing arguments. It sticks to the bare essentials. I have found that students and writers often need just such a list of reminders and rules, not lengthy introductory explanations. Thus, unlike most textbooks in argumentative writing or "informal logic," this book is organized around specific rules, illustrated and explained soundly but above all briefly. It is not a textbook but a *rule*book.

Instructors too, I have found, often wish to assign such a rulebook, a treatment that students can consult and understand on their own and that therefore does not intrude on classtime. Here again it is important to be brief—the point is to help students get on with writing a paper or with assessing an argument—but the rules must be stated with enough explanation that an instructor can simply refer a student to Rule 6 or Rule 16 rather than writing an entire explanation in the margins of each student's paper. Brief but self-sufficient—that is the fine line I have tried to follow.

This rulebook also can be used in a course that gives explicit attention to arguments. It will need to be supplemented with exercises and with more examples, but many texts are already available that consist largely or wholly of such exercises and examples. *Those* texts, however, also need to be supplemented—with what this rulebook offers: simple rules for putting good arguments together. Too many students come out of critical thinking courses knowing only how to shoot down (or at least *at*) selected fallacies. Too often they can't explain what is actually wrong, or launch an argument of their own. We can do better: this book is one attempt to suggest how.

Comments and criticisms are welcome.

Anthony Weston
August 1986

Note to the Third Edition

In this millennial reissue the most notable change is a more rule-oriented approach to the topic of definition. A long talk with Professor Charles Kay of Wofford College, close reader and attentive teacher, persuaded me to make this and a number of other changes. Many examples have been updated or clarified. Generous feedback from users too numerous to list continues to improve this little book—my thanks to you all.

A.W.
May 2000

Introduction

What's the Point of Arguing?

Some people think that arguing is simply stating their prejudices in a new form. This is why many people also think that
arguments are unpleasant and pointless. One dictionary definition for "argument" is "disputation." In this sense we sometimes say that two people "*have* an argument": a verbal
fistfight. It happens often enough. But it is not what arguments
really are.

In this book, "to give an argument" means *to offer a set of
reasons or evidence in support of a conclusion.* Here an argument is *not* simply a statement of certain views, and it is not
simply a dispute. Arguments are attempts to *support* certain
views with reasons. Nor are arguments in this sense pointless;
in fact, they are essential.

Argument is essential, in the first place, because it is a way of
trying to find out which views are better than others. Not all
views are equal. Some conclusions can be supported by good
reasons; others have much weaker support. But often we don't

know which are which. We need to give arguments for different conclusions and then assess those arguments to see how strong they really are.

Argument in this sense is a means of *inquiry*. Some philosophers and activists have argued, for instance, that the "factory farming" of animals for meat causes immense suffering to animals and is therefore unjustified and immoral. Are they right? You can't tell by consulting your prejudices. Many issues are involved. Do we have moral obligations to other species, for instance, or is only human suffering really bad? How well can humans live without meat? Some vegetarians have lived to very old ages. Does this show that vegetarian diets are healthier? Or is it irrelevant when you consider that some nonvegetarians also have lived to very old ages? (You might make some progress by asking whether a higher *percentage* of vegetarians live to old age.) Or might healthier people tend to become vegetarians, rather than vice versa? All of these questions need to be considered carefully, and the answers are not clear in advance.

Argument is essential for another reason too. Once we have arrived at a conclusion that is well-supported by reasons, argument is how we explain and *defend* it. A good argument doesn't merely repeat conclusions. Instead it offers reasons and evidence so that other people can make up their minds for themselves. If you become convinced that we should indeed change the way we raise and use animals, for example, you must use arguments to explain how you arrived at your conclusion. That is how you will convince others: by offering the reasons and evidence that convinced *you*. It is not a mistake to have strong views. The mistake is to have nothing else.

Understanding Argumentative Essays

The rules of argument, then, are not arbitrary; they have a specific purpose. But students (as well as other writers) do not always understand that purpose when first assigned argumentative essays—and if you don't understand an assignment, you are unlikely to do well on it. Many students, asked to argue for their views on some issue, write out elaborate *statements* of their views but do not offer any real *reasons* to think their views are correct. They write an essay, but not an argument.

This is a natural misunderstanding. In high school, the emphasis is on learning fairly clear-cut and uncontroversial subjects. You need not *argue* that the United States Constitution provides for three branches of government or that Shakespeare wrote *Macbeth*. You only need to master these facts, and your papers only need to report them.

Students may come to college expecting more of the same. But many college courses—especially those that assign writing—have a different aim. These courses are concerned with the *basis* of our beliefs; they require students to question their beliefs and to work out and defend their own views. The issues discussed in college courses are often not so clear-cut and certain. Yes, the Constitution provides for three branches of government, but should the Supreme Court really have veto power over the other two? Yes, Shakespeare wrote *Macbeth,* but what does the play mean? Reasons and evidence can be given for different answers. Students in these courses are asked to learn to think for themselves, to form their own views in a responsible way. The ability to defend your views is a measure of that skill, and that is why argumentative essays are so important.

In fact, as Chapters VII–IX will explain, to write a good argumentative essay you must use arguments *both* as a means of inquiry *and* as a way of explaining and defending your conclusions. You must prepare for the paper by exploring the arguments on the opposing sides. Then you must write the essay itself as an argument, defending your conclusions with arguments and critically assessing some of the arguments on the opposing sides.

Outline of This Book

This book begins by discussing fairly simple arguments and moves to argumentative essays at the end.

Chapters I–VI are about composing and assessing *short* arguments. A "short" argument simply offers its reasons and evidence briefly, usually in a few sentences or a paragraph.

We begin with short arguments for several reasons. First, they are common. In fact they are so common that they are part of every day's conversation. Second, long arguments are often elaborations of short arguments, or a series of short arguments linked together. If you learn to write and assess short arguments first, then you can extend your skills to argumentative essays.

A third reason for beginning with short arguments is that they are the best illustrations both of the common argument forms and of the typical mistakes in arguments. In long arguments it is harder to pick out the main points—and the main problems. Therefore, although some of the rules may seem obvious when first stated, remember that you have the benefit of a simple example. Other rules are hard enough to appreciate even in short arguments.

Chapters VII, VIII, and IX turn to argumentative essays. Chapter VII is about the first step: exploring the issue. Chapter VIII outlines the main points of an argumentative essay, and Chapter IX adds rules specifically about writing it. All of these chapters depend on Chapters I–VI, since an argumentative essay essentially combines and elaborates the kinds of short arguments that Chapters I–VI discuss. Don't skip ahead to the argumentative essay chapters, then, even if you come to this book primarily for help writing an essay. The book is short enough to read through to Chapters VII, VIII, and IX, and when you arrive there you will have the tools you need to use those chapters well. Instructors might wish to assign Chapters I–VI early in the term and Chapters VII–IX at essay-writing time.

Chapter X concerns fallacies, misleading arguments. It summarizes the general mistakes discussed in the rest of this book, and ends with a roster of the many misleading arguments that are so tempting and common that they even have their own names. The Appendix offers some rules for constructing and evaluating definitions.

I

Composing a Short Argument

Some General Rules

Chapter I offers some general rules for composing short arguments. Chapters II through VI discuss specific *kinds* of short arguments.

1. Distinguish premises and conclusion

The first step in making an argument is to ask, what are you trying to prove? What is your conclusion? Remember that the conclusion is the statement for which you are giving reasons. The statements that give your reasons are called *premises*.

Consider this quip of Winston Churchill's:

> Be an optimist. There is not much use being anything else.

This is an argument because Churchill is giving a *reason* to be an optimist: His premise is that "there is not much use being anything else."

Churchill's premise and conclusion are obvious enough, but the conclusions of some arguments may not be obvious until they are pointed out. Sherlock Holmes has to explain one of his key conclusions in "The Adventure of Silver Blaze":

> A dog was kept in the stalls, and yet, though someone had been
> in and fetched out a horse, the dog had not barked. Obviously the
> visitor was someone whom the dog knew well. . . .

Holmes has two premises. One is explicit: The dog did not bark
at the visitor. The other is a general fact he assumes we know
about dogs: Dogs bark at strangers. Together these premises
imply that the visitor was not a stranger.

When you are using arguments as a means of *inquiry,* as
described in the Introduction, you may sometimes start with no
more than the conclusion you wish to defend. State it clearly,
first of all. If you want to take Churchill at his word and argue
that we should indeed be optimists, say so explicitly. Then
ask yourself what reasons you have for drawing that conclusion. What reasons can you give to prove that we should be
optimists?

You could appeal to Churchill's authority: If Churchill says
we should be optimists, who are you and I to quibble? This
appeal will not get you very far, however, since probably an
equal number of famous people have recommended pessimism.
You need to think about it on your own. Again, what is *your*
reason for thinking that we should be optimists?

Maybe your idea is that being an optimist gives you more
energy to work for success, whereas pessimists feel defeated in
advance and never even try. Thus you have one main reason:
Optimists are more likely to succeed, to achieve their goals.
(Maybe this is what Churchill meant as well.) If this is your
reason, say so explicitly.

Once you have finished this book, you will have a ready list
of many of the different forms that arguments can take. Use
them to develop your premises. To defend a generalization, for
instance, check Chapter II. It will remind you that you need to
give a series of examples as premises, and it will tell you what
sorts of examples to look for. If your conclusion requires a
deductive argument like those explained in Chapter VI, the
rules discussed in that chapter will tell you what types of prem-

ises you need. You may have to try several different arguments before you find one that works well.

2. Present your ideas in a natural order

Short arguments are usually written in one or two paragraphs. Put the conclusion first, followed by your reasons, or set out your premises first and draw the conclusion at the end. In any case, set out your ideas in an order that unfolds your line of thought most naturally for the reader. Consider this short argument by Bertrand Russell:

> The evils of the world are due to moral defects quite as much as to lack of intelligence. But the human race has not hitherto discovered any method of eradicating moral defects. . . . Intelligence, on the contrary, is easily improved by methods known to every competent educator. Therefore, until some method of teaching virtue has been discovered, progress will have to be sought by improvement of intelligence rather than of morals.*

Each claim in this passage leads naturally to the next. Russell begins by pointing out the two sources of evil in the world: "moral defects," as he puts it, and lack of intelligence. He then claims that we do not know how to correct "moral defects," but that we do know how to correct lack of intelligence. Therefore—notice that the word "therefore" clearly marks his conclusion—progress will have to come by improving intelligence.

Each sentence in this argument is in just the right place. Plenty of wrong places were available. Suppose Russell instead wrote it like this:

---

* *Skeptical Essays* (1935; reprint, London: Allen and Unwin, 1977), p. 127.

The evils of the world are due to moral defects quite as much as lack of intelligence. Until some method of teaching virtue has been discovered, progress will have to be sought by improvement of intelligence rather than of morals. Intelligence is easily improved by methods known to every competent educator. But the human race has not hitherto discovered any means of eradicating moral defects.

These are exactly the same premises and conclusion, but they are in a different order, and the word "therefore" has been omitted before the conclusion. Now the argument is *much* harder to understand. The premises do not fit together naturally, and you have to read the passage twice just to figure out what the conclusion is. Don't count on your readers to be so patient.

Expect to rearrange your argument several times to find the most natural order. The rules discussed in this book should help. You can use them not only to tell what premises you need but also how to arrange your premises in the most natural order.

3.   Start from reliable premises

No matter how well you argue *from* premises to conclusion, your conclusion will be weak if your premises are weak.

Nobody in the world today is really happy. Therefore, it seems that human beings are just not made for happiness. Why should we expect what we can never find?

The premise of this argument is the statement that nobody in the world today is really happy. Ask yourself if this premise is plausible. Is *nobody* in the world today really happy? At the very least this premise needs some defense, and very likely it is just not true. This argument cannot show, then, that human beings are not made for happiness or that we should not expect to be happy.

Sometimes it is easy to start from reliable premises. You may have well-known examples at hand or informed authorities who are clearly in agreement. Other times it is harder. If you are not sure about the reliability of a premise, you may need to do some research and/or give a short argument for the premise itself. (We will return to this theme in later chapters, especially in Rule A2 of Chapter VII.) If you find you *cannot* argue adequately for your premise(s), then, of course, you need to give up entirely and start elsewhere!

4. Be concrete and concise

Avoid abstract, vague, and general terms. "We hiked for hours in the sun" is a hundred times better than "It was an extended period of laborious exertion." Be concise too. Airy elaboration just loses everyone—even the writer—in a fog of words.

NO:

For those whose roles primarily involved the performance of services, as distinguished from assumption of leadership respon-sibilities, the main pattern seems to have been a response to the leadership's invoking obligations that were concomitants of the status of membership in the societal community and various of its segmental units. The closest modern analogy is the military ser-vice performed by an ordinary citizen, except that the leader of the Egyptian bureaucracy did not need a special emergency to invoke legitimate obligations.*

---

* This passage is from Talcott Parsons, *Societies: Evolutionary and Comparative Perspectives* (Englewood Cliffs, NJ: Prentice Hall, 1966), p. 56. I owe the quotation and the rewritten version that follows to Stanislas Andreski, *Social Sciences as Sorcery* (New York: St. Martin's Press, 1972), Chapter 6.

YES:

In ancient Egypt the common people were liable to be conscripted for work.

5. Avoid loaded language

Do not make your argument look good by mocking or distorting the other side. Generally, people advocate a position for serious and sincere reasons. Try to figure out their view—try to get it *right*—even if you disagree entirely. A person who questions a new technology is not in favor of "going back to the caves," for example, and a person who believes in evolution is not claiming that her grandma was a monkey. If you can't imagine how anyone could hold the view you are attacking, you just don't understand it yet.

In general, avoid language whose only function is to sway the emotions. This is "loaded language."

Having so disgracefully allowed her once-proud passenger railroads to fade into obscurity, America is honor bound to restore them now!

This is supposed to be an argument for restoring (more) passenger rail service. But it offers no evidence for this conclusion whatsoever, just some emotionally loaded words—shopworn words, too, like a politician on automatic. Did passenger rail "fade" because of something "America" did or didn't do? What was "disgraceful" about this? Many "once-proud" institutions fall into disarray, after all—we're not obliged to restore them all. What does it mean to say America is "honor bound" to do this? Have promises been made and broken? By whom?

Much can be said for restoring passenger rail, especially in this era when the ecological and economic costs of highways are becoming enormous. The problem here is that this argument does not say it. It lets the overtones of the words do all the work, and therefore really does no work at all. We're left exactly where we started. When it's your turn, stick to the evidence.

6. Use consistent terms

Arguments depend on clear connections between their premises and between premises and conclusion. For this reason it is vital to use a single set of terms for each idea.

NO:

If you study other cultures, then you realize the variety of human customs. If you understand the diversity of social practices, then you question your own customs. If you acquire doubts about the way you do things, then you become more tolerant. Therefore, if you expand your knowledge of anthropology, then you become more likely to accept other people and practices without criticism.

YES:

If you study other cultures, then you realize the variety of human customs. If you realize the variety of human customs, then you question your own customs. If you question your own customs, then you become more tolerant. Therefore, if you study other cultures, then you become more tolerant.

Notice that in both versions, each of the sentences has the form "If X, then Y." But now look at the differences.

The second ("Yes") version is crystal clear—because the Y of each premise is exactly the X of the next. The Y of the first is exactly the X of the second, the Y of the second is exactly the X of the third, and so on. (Go back and look.) This is why the argument is so easy to read and understand: It forms a kind of chain.

In the first ("No") version, though, the Y of the first premise is only roughly the X of the second, the Y of the second premise is only roughly the X of the third, and so on. Here each X and Y is written as if the author had consulted the thesaurus at every opportunity. "More tolerant," in the third premise, for instance, is written as "more likely to accept other people and practices without criticism" in the conclusion. As a result, the argument loses the obvious connection between its parts that could make it clear and persuasive. The writer shows off, but the reader— who is not privileged to know the structure of the argument from the start—just flounders.

7.   Stick to one meaning for each term

Some arguments slide from one meaning of a term to another to make their case. This is the classical fallacy of *equivocation:*

> Women and men are physically and emotionally different. The sexes are *not* "equal," then, and therefore the law should not pretend that we are!

This argument may seem plausible at first glance, but between premise and conclusion it moves between two very different senses of the term "equal." True enough, the sexes are not physically and emotionally "equal" in the sense in which "equal" means simply "identical." "Equality" before the *law,* however, does not mean "physically and emotionally identical" but "entitled to the same rights and opportunities." Rephrased, then, with the two different senses of "equal" made clear, the argument goes:

> Women and men are not physically and emotionally identical. Therefore, women and men are not entitled to the same rights and opportunities.

This version of the argument no longer equivocates on "equal," but it is still not a good argument; it is only the original inadequate argument with the inadequacy no longer hidden. Once the equivocation is removed, it is clear that the argument's conclusion is neither supported by nor even related to the premise. No reason is offered to show that physical and emotional differences should have anything to do with rights and opportunities.

Sometimes we are tempted to equivocate by making a key word *vague*. Consider the following conversation:

> A: Everyone is really just selfish!
>
> B: But what about John? Look how he devotes himself to his children!
>
> A: He is only doing what he really wants to do—that's still selfish!

Here the meaning of "selfish" changes from A's first claim to A's second. In the first claim, we understand "selfish" to mean something fairly specific: the grasping, self-centered behavior we ordinarily call "selfish." In A's response to B's objection, A expands the meaning of "selfish" to include apparently unselfish behavior too, by broadening the definition to just "doing what you really want to do." A saves only the *word;* it has lost its original meaning.

A good way to avoid equivocation is to carefully *define* any key terms when you introduce them. Then be sure to use them only as you've defined them! You also may need to define special terms or technical words. See the Appendix for a discussion of the process and pitfalls of definition.

II

Arguments by Example

Arguments by example offer one or more specific examples in support of a generalization.

> Women in earlier times were married very young. Juliet in Shakespeare's *Romeo and Juliet* was not even fourteen years old. In the Middle Ages thirteen was the normal age of marriage for a Jewish woman. And during the Roman Empire many Roman women were married while thirteen or younger.

This argument generalizes from three examples—Juliet, Jewish women in the Middle Ages, and Roman women during the Roman Empire—to "many" or *most* women in earlier times. To show the form of this argument most clearly, we can list the premises separately, with the conclusion on the "bottom line":

> Juliet in Shakespeare's play was not even fourteen years old.
> Jewish women during the Middle Ages were normally married at thirteen.
> Many Roman women during the Roman Empire were married while thirteen or younger.
> Therefore, many women in earlier times were married very young.

Often I will write short arguments in this way when it is important to see exactly how they work.

When do premises like these adequately support a generalization?

One requirement, of course, is that the examples be accurate. Remember Rule 3: An argument must start from reliable premises! If Juliet *wasn't* around fourteen, or if most Roman or Jewish women *weren't* married at thirteen or younger, then the argument is much weaker, and if none of the premises can be supported, there is no argument at all. To check an argument's examples, or to find good examples for your own arguments, you may need to do some research.

But suppose the examples *are* accurate. Generalizing from them is still a tricky business. Chapter II offers a short checklist for assessing arguments by example—both your own and others'.

8.   Give more than one example

A single example can sometimes be used for the sake of *illustration*. The example of Juliet alone might illustrate early marriage. But a single example offers next to no *support* for a generalization. More than one example is needed.

NO:

Women's rights to vote were won only after a struggle.

Therefore, all women's rights are won only after a struggle.

YES:

Women's rights to vote were won only after a struggle.

Women's rights to attend colleges and universities were won only after a struggle.

Women's rights to equal employment opportunity are being won only after a struggle.

Therefore, all women's rights are won only after a struggle.

In a generalization about a small set of things, the best argument considers all, or nearly all, the examples. A generalization about all American presidents since Kennedy should consider each of them in turn. Likewise, the argument that women's rights always have required struggles should consider all, or most, important rights.

Generalizations about larger sets of things require picking out a "sample." We certainly cannot list all women in earlier times who married young; instead, our argument must offer a few women as examples of the rest. How many examples are required depends partly on their representativeness, a point Rule 9 takes up. It also depends partly on the size of the set being generalized about. Large sets usually require more examples. The claim that your town is full of remarkable people requires more evidence than the claim that, say, your *friends* are remarkable people. Depending on how many friends you have, even just two or three examples might be enough to establish that your friends are remarkable people, but unless your town is tiny, many more examples are required to show that your town is full of remarkable people.

9. Use representative examples

Even a large number of examples may *misrepresent* the set being generalized about. A large number of examples of Roman women alone, for instance, might establish very little about women generally, since Roman women are not necessarily representative of women in other parts of the world. The argument needs to consider women from other parts of the world as well.

> Everyone in my neighborhood favors McGraw for president. Therefore, McGraw is sure to win.

This argument is weak because single neighborhoods seldom represent the voting population as a whole. A well-to-do neighborhood may favor a candidate who is unpopular with everyone else. Student wards in university towns regularly are carried by candidates who do poorly elsewhere. Besides, we seldom have good evidence even about neighborhood views. The set of people who put signs in their yards and stickers on their cars (and whose lawns are visible from busy roads or who drive regularly and/or park their cars in noticeable locations) may well misrepresent the neighborhood as a whole.

A *good* argument that "McGraw is sure to win" requires a representative sample of the entire voting population. It is not easy to construct such a sample. Public-opinion polls, for instance, construct their samples very carefully. They learned the hard way. In 1936, the *Literary Digest* conducted the first large-scale public opinion poll, predicting the outcome of the presidential contest between Roosevelt and Landon. Names were taken, as they are now, from telephone listings, and also from automobile registration lists. The number of people polled was certainly not too small: more than two million "ballots" were counted. The poll predicted a wide victory for Landon. Roosevelt, however, won easily. In retrospect it is easy to see what went wrong. In 1936 only a select portion of the population owned telephones and cars. The sample was sharply biased toward wealthy and urban voters, more of whom supported Landon.*

Polls have improved since then. Nonetheless, there are worries about the representativeness of their samples, particularly when the samples are small. Nearly everyone now has a telephone, to be sure, but some people have more than one; many others have unlisted numbers; some numbers represent a whole household of voters and others only one; some people are unwilling to talk to pollsters; and so on. Even carefully selected

---

* Mildred Parten, *Surveys, Polls, and Samples* (New York: Harper and Row, 1950), pp. 25, 290, 393–5. Parten also shows that lower income people, who were less likely to receive "ballots" than wealthy people, were less likely to return them, too.

samples, then, may be unrepresentative. Many of the best polls, for instance, badly miscalled the 1980 presidential election.

The representativeness of any given sample, then, is always somewhat uncertain. Anticipate this danger! Look for samples that represent the whole population being generalized about. If you want to know how much television children watch, don't just survey the third graders at your local public school. If you want to know what people in other countries think about the United States, don't just ask tourists.

Do some research. Juliet, for example, is just one woman. Is she representative even of women in her time and place? In Shakespeare's play, Juliet's mother says to her:

> Think of marriage now; younger than you,
> Here in Verona, ladies of esteem,
> Are made already mothers. By my count,
> I was your mother much upon these years
> That you are now a maid . . .
>
> (1.3.69–73)

This passage suggests that Juliet's marriage at fourteen is not exceptional; in fact, fourteen seems to be a little on the old side.

When making your own argument, do not rely only on examples that come "off the top of your head." The sorts of examples you think of at a moment's notice are likely to be biased. Again, do some reading, think about the appropriate sample carefully, and keep yourself honest by looking for counterexamples (Rule 11).

10.   Background information is crucial

We often need *background information* before we can assess a set of examples.

> You should use Slapdash Services—we already have dozens of completely satisfied customers in your area!

Slapdash may indeed have "dozens" of "completely" satisfied customers in your area—although this sort of claim is often made without any evidence at all—but you also need to consider how many people in your area have *tried* Slapdash. If a thousand people have tried Slapdash and two dozen are satisfied, then, although there are indeed "dozens" of satisfied customers, Slapdash satisfies only 2.4 percent of its customers. Try somewhere else.

Here is another example.

> The "Bermuda Triangle" area off Bermuda is famous as a place where many ships and planes have mysteriously disappeared. There have been several dozen disappearances in the past decade alone.

No doubt. But "several dozen" out of how many ships and planes that *passed through* the area? Several dozen or several tens of thousands? If only several dozen have disappeared out of (say) twenty thousand, then the disappearance rate in the Bermuda Triangle may well be normal or even low—certainly not mysterious.

Consider how often, when buying a car or selecting a school, we are swayed by the reports of a few friends or one or two experiences of our own. Hearing about someone's sister-in-law who had a terrible time with her Volvo is enough to keep us from buying a Volvo—even though *Consumer Reports* might indicate that Volvos are generally very reliable cars. We let one vivid example outweigh the careful summary and comparison of thousands of repair records. Richard Nisbett and Lee Ross term this the "person who" argument,* as in "I know a *person who* smoked three packs of cigarettes a day and lived to be 100"

---

* See *Human Inference: Strategies and Shortcomings of Social Judgment* (Englewood Cliffs, NJ: Prentice Hall, 1980), p. 61. Actually, they call it the "man who" argument; I have universalized the language.

or "I know a *person who* had a Volvo that was a real lemon." It is nearly always a fallacy. As Nisbett and Ross point out, one car that turns out to be a lemon changes the frequency-of-repair rates only slightly.

To judge a set of examples, then, we often need to consider background *rates.* Correspondingly, when an argument offers rates or percentages, the relevant background information usually must include the *number* of examples. Car thefts on campus may have increased 100 percent, but if this means that two cars were stolen rather than one, not much has changed.

Here is one last example:

> After an era when some athletic powerhouse universities were accused of exploiting student athletes, leaving them to flunk out once their eligibility expired, college athletes are now graduating at higher rates. At many schools their graduation rate is more than 50 percent.

Fifty percent, eh? Pretty impressive! But this figure, at first so persuasive, does not really do the job it claims to do.

First, though "many" schools graduate more than 50 percent of their athletes, it appears that some do not—so this figure may well exclude the most exploitative schools that really concerned people in the first place.

Second, it would be useful to know how a "more than 50 percent" graduation rate compares with the graduation rate for *all* students at the same institutions. If it is significantly lower, athletes may still be getting the shaft.

Finally and perhaps most important, this argument offers no reason to believe that college athletes' graduation rates are actually *improving*—because no *comparison* to any previous rate is offered. Maybe we had the impression athletes' graduation rates used to be lower, but without knowing the previous rates it is impossible to tell!

11. Consider counterexamples

Test generalizations by asking if there are counterexamples.

> The Peloponnesian War was caused by the Athenians' desire to dominate Greece.
>
> The Napoleonic Wars were caused by Napoleon's desire to dominate Europe.
>
> World War II was caused by the Fascists' desire to dominate Europe.
>
> Thus, in general, wars are caused by the desire for territorial domination.

Are *all* wars, however, caused by the desire for territorial domination? Or might this generalization go too far beyond its examples?

In fact, there are counterexamples. Revolutions, for example, have quite different causes. So do civil wars.

If you can think of counterexamples to a generalization that you want to defend, revise your generalization. If the above argument were yours, for instance, you might change the conclusion to "Wars *between independent states* are caused by the desire for territorial domination." Even this may overgeneralize, but at least it's more defensible than the original.

Other times you may want to dispute the supposed counterexample. World War I, someone may object, seems to have been caused not by the desire for territorial domination but by a network of mutual defense pacts and other political intrigues, by the restlessness of the European upper classes, by nationalist unrest in Eastern Europe, and so on. In the face of this example, you might, of course, give up your claim entirely or weaken it still further. Another response, however, is to argue that the supposed counterexample actually does conform to the generalization. After all (you might argue), the desires of the European powers to dominate Europe were the *motives* for the mutual defense pacts and other intrigues that finally set off the war.

And might not nationalist unrest, too, be caused by unjust domination presently in place? Here, in effect, you try to reinterpret the *counter*example as another *example*. The initial challenge to your conclusion becomes another piece of evidence for it. You may or may not change the phrasing of your conclusion: In any case, you now understand your claim better, and you are prepared to answer an important objection.

Also try to think of counterexamples when you are assessing others' arguments. Ask whether *their* conclusions might have to be revised and limited, whether perhaps those conclusions might have to be given up entirely, or whether a supposed counterexample might be reinterpreted as another example. The same rules apply to anyone else's arguments as apply to yours. The only difference is that you have a chance to correct your overgeneralizations yourself.

III

Arguments by Analogy

There is an exception to Rule 8 ("Give more than one example"). *Arguments by analogy,* rather than multiplying examples to support a generalization, argue from *one* specific case or example to another example, reasoning that because the two examples are alike in many ways they are also alike in one further specific way.

For example, here is how a medical administrator argues that everyone should have a regular physical checkup:

> People take in their car for servicing and checkups every few months without complaint. Why shouldn't they take similar care of their bodies?*

This argument suggests that getting a regular physical checkup is *like* taking your car in for regular servicing. Cars need that kind of attention—otherwise, major problems may develop. Well, says Dr. Beary, our bodies are like that too.

---

* Dr. John Beary III, quoted in "News You Can Use," *U.S. News and World Report,* 11 August 1986, p. 61.

People should take their cars in for regular service and check-ups (otherwise major problems may develop).

People's bodies are *like* cars (because human bodies, too, can develop problems if not regularly checked up).

Therefore, people should take themselves in for regular "service" and checkups too.

Notice the italicized word "like" in the second premise. When an argument stresses the likeness between two cases, it is very probably an argument from analogy.

Here is a more complex example.

An interesting switch was pulled in Rome yesterday by Adam Nordwell, an American Chippewa chief. As he descended his plane from California dressed in full tribal regalia, Nordwell announced in the name of the American Indian people that he was taking possession of Italy "by right of discovery" in the same way that Christopher Columbus did in America. "I proclaim this day the day of the discovery of Italy," said Nordwell. "What right did Columbus have to discover America when it had already been inhabited for thousands of years? The same right I now have to come to Italy and proclaim the discovery of your country."*

Nordwell is suggesting that his "discovery" of Italy is *like* Columbus's "discovery" of America in at least one important way: Both Nordwell and Columbus claimed a country that already had been inhabited by its own people for centuries. Thus Nordwell insists that he has as much "right" to claim Italy as Columbus had to claim America. But, of course, Nordwell has no right at all to claim Italy. Therefore, Columbus had no right at all to claim America.

---

* *Miami News,* 23 September 1973.

Nordwell has no right to claim Italy for another people, let alone "by right of discovery" (because Italy has been inhabited by its own people for centuries).

Columbus's claim to America "by right of discovery" is *like* Nordwell's claim to Italy (America, too, had been inhabited by its own people for centuries).

Therefore, Columbus had no right to claim America for another people, let alone "by right of discovery."

How do we evaluate arguments by analogy?

The first premise of an argument by analogy makes a claim about the example used as an analogy. Remember Rule 3: make sure this premise is true. It's true that cars need regular service and checkups to keep major problems from developing, for instance, and it's true that Adam Nordwell could not claim Italy for the Chippewa.

The second premise in arguments by analogy claims that the example in the first premise is *like* the example about which the argument draws a conclusion. Evaluating this premise is harder, and needs a rule of its own.

12. Analogy requires a relevantly similar example

Analogies do not require that the example used as an analogy be *exactly* like the example in the conclusion. Our bodies are not just like cars, after all. We are flesh and bone rather than metal, we last longer, and so on. Analogies require *relevant* similarities. What cars are made of is irrelevant to Dr. Beary's point; his argument is about the upkeep of complex systems.

One relevant difference between our bodies and our cars is that our bodies do not need regular "service" in the way our cars do. Cars need service to replace or replenish certain parts and fluids: oil changes, new pumps or transmissions, and the like. Our bodies don't. Replacing parts or fluids is much rarer and is more like surgery or blood transfusion, not regular "servicing" at all. Still, it's probably true that we need regular checkups—

otherwise problems can develop undetected. So the doctor's analogy is only partly successful. The "service" part makes a poor analogy, though the checkup part is persuasive.

Likewise, twentieth-century Italy is not just like fifteenth-century America. Italy is known to every twentieth-century schoolchild, for instance, whereas in the fifteenth century America was unknown to much of the world. Nordwell is not an explorer, and a commercial jet is not the *Santa Maria*.

Nordwell suggests, however, that these differences are not relevant to his analogy. Nordwell simply means to remind us that it is senseless to claim a country already inhabited by its own people. Whether that land is known to the world's schoolchildren, or how the "discoverer" arrived there, is not important. The more appropriate reaction might have been to try to establish diplomatic relations, as we would try to do today if somehow the land and people of Italy had just been discovered. *That's* Nordwell's point, and taken in that way his analogy makes a good argument.

One famous argument uses an analogy to try to establish the existence of a Creator of the world. We can infer the existence of a Creator from the order and beauty of the world, this argument claims, just as we can infer the existence of an architect or carpenter when we see a beautiful and well-built house. Spelled out in premise-and-conclusion form:

> Beautiful and well-built houses must have "makers": intelligent designers and builders.
>
> The world is *like* a beautiful and well-built house.
>
> Therefore, the world also must have a "maker": an intelligent Designer and Builder, God.

Again, more examples are not needed here; the argument wishes to stress the similarity of the world to *one* example, a house.

Whether the world really *is* relevantly similar to a house, though, is not so clear. We know quite a bit about the causes of houses. But houses are *parts* of nature. We know very little, actually, about the structure of nature as a *whole* or about what sort of causes it might be expected to have. David Hume discussed this argument in his *Dialogues Concerning Natural Religion* and asked:

> Is *part* of nature a rule for the whole? . . . Think [of how] wide a step you have taken when you compared houses . . . to the universe, and from their similarity in some circumstances inferred a similarity in their causes. . . . Does not the great disproportion bar all comparison and inference?*

The world is different from a house in at least this: A house is part of a larger whole, the world, while the world itself (the universe) is the largest of wholes. Thus Hume suggests that the universe is *not* relevantly similar to a house. Houses indeed imply "makers" beyond themselves, but—for all we know—the universe as a whole may contain its cause within itself. This analogy, then, makes a poor argument. Some other kind of argument is probably needed if the existence of God is to be inferred from the nature of the world.

---

* David Hume, *Dialogues Concerning Natural Religion* (1779; reprint, Indianapolis: Hackett Publishing Company, 1980), Part II.

IV

Arguments from Authority

No one can become an expert, through direct experience, on everything there is to know. We cannot taste every wine in the world to determine which is best. We cannot know what the trial of Socrates was really like. We are unlikely to know firsthand what is happening in the state legislature, Sri Lanka, or outer space. Instead, we must rely on others—better-situated people, organizations, or reference works—to tell us much of what we need to know about the world. We need what are called *arguments from authority*.

> X (a source that ought to know) says Y.
>
> Therefore, Y is true.

For instance:

> My friend Marcos says Greek wines are the best in the world.
>
> Therefore, Greek wines are the best in the world.

But relying on others also can be a risky business. Everyone has their biases. Supposed authorities may mislead us, or may be misled themselves, or may miss key parts of the big picture. Once again we must consider a checklist of requirements that good arguments from authority must meet.

13.   Sources should be cited

Factual assertions not otherwise defended may be supported by reference to the appropriate sources. Some factual assertions, of course, are so obvious that they do not need support at all. It is usually not necessary to *prove* that the population of the United States is more than 200 million or that Juliet loved Romeo. However, a precise figure for the population of the United States or, say, for the current rate of population growth *does* need a citation. Likewise, the claim that Juliet was only fourteen should cite a few Shakespearean lines in support.

NO:

   I once read that there are cultures in which makeup and clothes are mostly men's business.

If you're arguing about whether men and women everywhere follow the same sorts of gender roles as in the United States, this is a relevant example—a striking case of different gender roles. But it's probably not the sort of difference you have experienced yourself. To nail down the argument, you need to go back and find your source, check it out again, and cite it.

YES:

   Carol Beckwith, in "Niger's Wodaabe" (*National Geographic* 164, no. 4 [October 1983]: 483–509), reports that among the West African Fulani peoples such as the Wodaabe, makeup and clothes are mostly men's business.

Citation styles vary—you may need a handbook of style to find the appropriate style for your purposes—but all include the same basic information: enough so that others can easily find the source on their own.

14. Seek informed sources

Sources must be *qualified* to make the statements they make. The Census Bureau is entitled to make claims about the population of the United States. Auto mechanics are qualified to discuss the merits of different automobiles, doctors are qualified on matters of medicine, ecologists on the environmental effects of pollution, and so on. These sources are qualified because they have the appropriate background and information.

Where an authority's background or information are not immediately clear, an argument must explain them briefly. The argument cited in Rule 13, for example, might need to be expanded further:

> Carol Beckwith, in "Niger's Wodaabe" (*National Geographic* 164, no. 4 [October 1983]: 483–509), reports that among the West African Fulani peoples such as the Wodaabe, makeup and clothes are mostly men's business. Beckwith and an anthropologist colleague lived with the Wodaabe for two years and observed many dances for which the men prepared by lengthy preening, face-painting, and teeth-whitening. (Her article includes many pictures too.) Wodaabe women watch, comment, and choose mates for their beauty—which the men say is the natural way. "Our beauty makes the women want us," one says.

A person who has lived with the Wodaabe for two years is indeed qualified to report on their everyday practices. Notice that she also cites their own words in turn—for ultimately, of course, the best authorities on Wodaabe practice are the Wodaabe themselves.

An informed source need not fit our general stereotype of "an authority"—and a person who fits our stereotype of an authority may not even be an informed source.

NO:

President Bernard of Topheavy College told parents and re-
porters today that classrooms at Topheavy promote lively and
free exchange of ideas. Therefore, classrooms at Topheavy do
indeed promote lively and free exchange of ideas.

The president of a college may know very little about what
happens in its classrooms.

YES:

An accreditation committee's tabulation of all student course
evaluations for the past three years at Topheavy College shows
that only 5 percent of all students answered "Yes" when asked
whether classes at Topheavy promoted lively and free exchange
of ideas. Therefore, classes at Topheavy seldom promote lively
and free exchange of ideas.

In this case, students are the most informed sources.
Note that authorities on one subject are not necessarily informed about every subject on which they offer opinions.

Einstein was a pacifist; therefore pacifism must be right.

Einstein's genius in physics does not establish him as a genius
in political philosophy.
Sometimes, of course, we must rely on authorities whose
knowledge is better than ours but still less than perfect. For
example, governments or others sometimes try to limit the information we can get about what is happening in a war zone or
a political trial. The best information we can get may be
fragmentary—through international human rights organizations like Amnesty International, for example. If you must rely
on an authority with imperfect knowledge, acknowledge the
problem. Let your readers or hearers decide whether imperfect
authority is better than none at all.

Finally, beware of supposed authorities who claim to know what they could not possibly know. If a book claims to be "written as if the author had been a fly on the wall of the most closely guarded room in the Pentagon,"* you can reasonably guess that it is a book full of conjecture, gossip, rumors, and other untrustworthy information (unless, of course, the author really *was* a fly on the wall of the most closely guarded room in the Pentagon). Similarly, religious moralists often have declared that certain practices are wrong because they are contrary to the will of God. We should reply that God ought to be spoken for a little more cautiously. God's will is not easy to ascertain, and when God speaks so softly it is easy to confuse that "still small voice" with our own personal prejudices.

15. Seek impartial sources

People who have the most at stake in a dispute are usually not the best sources of information about the issues involved. Sometimes they may not even tell the truth. The person accused in a criminal trial is presumed innocent until proven guilty, but we seldom completely believe his or her claim to be innocent without confirmation from impartial witnesses. But even a willingness to tell the truth as one sees it is not always enough. The truth as one honestly sees it still can be biased. We tend to see what we expect to see: We notice, remember, and pass on information that supports our point of view, but we are not quite so motivated when the evidence points the other way.

Don't just rely on the president, then, if the issue is the effectiveness of the administration's policies. Don't just rely on the government for the best information on the human rights situation in countries the government happens to support or oppose. Don't just rely on interest groups on *one* side of a major public question for the most accurate information on the issues

---

* Advertisement in *New York Times Book Review,* 9 December 1984, p. 3.

at stake. Don't just rely on a product's manufacturer for the best information concerning that product.

NO:

Ads for Energizer batteries claim that Energizers are significantly better than other batteries. Therefore, Energizers are significantly better than other batteries.

Sources should be impartial. The best information on consumer products comes from the independent consumer magazines and testing agencies, because these agencies are unaffiliated with any manufacturer and must answer to consumers who want the most accurate information they can get.

YES:

Consumer Reports tested a variety of batteries and found no significant differences between them for nearly all uses (see "Who Sells the Best Cells?" *Consumer Reports,* December 1999, pp. 51–3). Therefore, Energizers are not significantly better than other batteries.

Likewise, independent servicepeople and mechanics are relatively impartial sources of information. An organization like Amnesty International is an impartial source on the human rights situation in other countries because it is not trying to support or oppose any specific government. On political matters, so long as the disagreements are basically over statistics, look to independent government agencies, such as the Census Bureau, or to university studies or other independent sources.

Make sure the source is *genuinely* independent and not just an interest group masquerading under an independent-sounding name. Check their sources of funding; check their other publications; and check the tone of the quoted report or book. At the very least, try to confirm for yourself any factual claim quoted from a potentially biased source. Good arguments cite their sources (Rule 13); look them up. Make sure the evidence is

quoted correctly and not pulled out of context, and check for
further information that might be relevant. You are then entitled
to cite those sources yourself.

16.   Cross-check sources

When experts disagree, you cannot rely on any one of them
alone. Before you quote any person or organization as an authority, you should check to make sure other equally qualified
and impartial people or organizations agree. One strength of
Amnesty International's reports, for instance, is that they usually are corroborated by reports from other independent human
rights monitoring organizations. (Again, they often *conflict*
with the reports of governments, but governments are seldom
so impartial.)

Authorities agree chiefly on specific factual questions. That
Wodaabe men spend a great deal of time on clothes and makeup
is a specific factual claim, for instance, and in principle is not
hard to verify. But as for larger and more intangible issues, it is
harder to find authorities who agree. On many philosophical
issues it is difficult to quote anyone as an uncontested expert.
Aristotle disagreed with Plato, Hegel with Kant. You may be
able to use their *arguments,* then, but no philosopher will be
convinced if you merely quote another philosopher's
conclusions.

17.   Personal attacks do not disqualify a source

Supposed authorities may be disqualified if they are not informed, impartial, or largely in agreement. Other sorts of attacks on authorities are not legitimate.

These are often called *ad hominem* fallacies: attacks on the
person of an authority rather than his or her specific qualifications to make the claim in question. If someone discounts a
supposed authority simply because they don't like the person—
don't like fundamentalists or Japanese or lesbians or rich peo-

ple or whatever it is—they are probably making this mistake. Normally a person's nationality, religion, sexual orientation, and so on, are irrelevant to their authority on specific factual questions within their expertise.

NO:

It's no surprise Carl Sagan claims that life is possible on Mars—after all, he's a well-known atheist. I don't believe it for a minute.

Sagan was an astronomer and a designer of interplanetary probes, and did extensive research on the question of life on Mars. Though he also took part in the public discussion about religion and science, there is no reason to think that his views about religion colored his scientific judgment about Martian life. If you don't like his conclusion, just criticize it directly.

V

Arguments about Causes

Do chills cause colds? Does Vitamin C prevent them? Does regular sex shorten life (as people once thought) or lengthen it (as some people now think) or make no difference to lifespan? How about regular exercise? What causes some people to become open-minded? to become geniuses? insomniacs? Republicans?

These are all questions about *causes* and their effects—about what causes what. They're vital questions. Good effects we want to increase; bad effects we want to prevent. Sometimes we need to figure out who or what caused something in order to give credit or lay blame. And sometimes we do it just to understand the world better.

The evidence for a claim about causes is usually a *correlation* between two events or kinds of events. Suppose, for instance, you wonder why some of your friends are more open-minded than others. You talk to your friends and discover that most of the open-minded ones are also well read—they keep up with newspapers, read literature, and so on—while most of the less open-minded ones are not. You discover, in other words, that there is a correlation between being well read and being open-minded. Then, because being well read seems to be *correlated* with open-mindedness, you might conclude that being well read *leads* to open-mindedness.

Arguments from correlation to cause are widely used in the medical and social sciences. To find out whether eating a full breakfast improves health, doctors do a study to find out whether people who usually eat a full breakfast live longer than people who usually don't. To find out whether reading really does tend to make a person more open-minded, a psychologist might devise a test for open-mindedness and a survey of reading habits, give the tests to a representative sample of the population, and then check to see whether a higher proportion of the regular readers are also open-minded.

Formal tests like these usually enter our arguments as arguments from authority: We rely on the authority of the people who did the tests, looking to their credentials and to their professional colleagues to make sure they are informed and impartial. We do have an obligation, however, to read and report their studies carefully and to try to assess them as best we can.

Our own arguments about causes usually have less carefully selected examples. We may argue from some striking cases in our own experience or from our knowledge of our friends or of history. These arguments are often speculative—but then, so are their more formal cousins that come from doctors and psychologists. Sometimes it is very difficult to know what causes what. This chapter offers several rules for any argument about causes and then a set of reminders about the pitfalls of moving from correlation to cause.

18.   Explain how cause leads to effect

When we think that A causes B, we usually believe not only that A and B are correlated but also that it "makes sense" for A to cause B. Good arguments, then, do not just appeal to the correlation of A and B: they also explain *why* it makes sense for A to cause B.

NO:

Most of my open-minded friends are well read; most of my
less open-minded friends are not. Reading, therefore, leads to
open-mindedness.

YES:

Most of my open-minded friends are well read; most of my
less open-minded friends are not. It seems likely that the more
you read, the more you encounter challenging new ideas, ideas
that make you less confident of your own. Reading also lifts you
out of your daily world and shows you how different and many-
sided life can be. Reading, therefore, leads to open-mindedness.

This argument could be more specific, but it does fill in some
important connections between cause and effect.

More formal and statistical arguments about causes—in
medicine, for example—also must try to fill in the connections
between the causes and the effects they postulate. Doctors don't
stop with evidence that merely demonstrates that eating a full
breakfast is correlated with improved health; they also want to
know *why* eating a full breakfast improves health.

Doctors N. B. Belloc and L. Breslow, respectively of the Human Population Laboratory of the California Department of Public Health and of the Department of Preventive and Social Medicine at UCLA, followed 7,000 adults for five and a half years,
relating life expectancy and health to certain basic health habits.
They found that eating a full breakfast is correlated with greater
life expectancy. (See Belloc and Breslow, "The Relation of Physical Health Status and Health Practices," *Preventive Medicine* 1
[August 1972]: 409–21.) It seems probable that people who eat a
full breakfast get more of the necessary nutrients than people who
skip breakfast or go through the morning on snacks and coffee. It
is also likely that if the body starts out the day with a good meal, it
metabolizes later meals more efficiently. Thus, it seems likely
that eating a full breakfast leads to better health.

Notice that this argument not only explains how cause may lead to effect but also cites its source and explains why that source is an informed source.

19. Propose the most likely cause

Most events have many possible causes. Just finding a possible cause, then, is not enough; you must go on to show that it is the most *likely* cause. It is always possible that the Bermuda Triangle really is inhabited by supernatural beings who protect their domain from human intrusion. It's *possible*. But the supernatural explanation is highly unlikely compared to the other likely explanations for the disappearance of ships and planes: tropical storms, unpredictable wind and wave patterns, and so on (if, indeed, anything *is* unusual about the Bermuda Triangle at all—remember Rule 10). Only if these everyday explanations fail to account for the facts should we begin to consider alternative hypotheses.

Likewise, it is always possible that people become open-minded, or at least tolerant, because they are just tired of arguing. Maybe they just want to "let the long contention cease." It's *possible*. But we also know that not very many people are like that. Most people who have dogmatic views stick up for them; it pains them too much to see other people going astray. Therefore, it seems more likely that people who become tolerant have truly become open-minded, and reading remains a likely cause.

How do we know which explanations are most likely? One rule of thumb is this: Prefer explanations compatible with our best-established beliefs. Natural science is well established; so is our ordinary understanding of what people are like. Of course, the explanation that seems most likely based on currently well-established beliefs still may turn out to be wrong. But we've got to start somewhere. Well-established beliefs are the least unreliable starting points we've got.

Sometimes additional evidence is necessary before *any* explanation can be accepted with much confidence. More evi-

dence is necessary when several competing "natural" explanations all fit the available evidence. Rules 20–23 explain some of
the most common types of competing explanations.

20.   Correlated events are not necessarily related

Some correlations are just coincidental.

> Ten minutes after I took Doctor Hartshorne's Insomnia Bitters,
> I was sound asleep. Therefore, Doctor Hartshorne's Insomnia
> Bitters put me to sleep.

Here the event being explained is my going to sleep. Because
my going to sleep was correlated with my taking Doctor
Hartshorne's Insomnia Bitters, the argument concludes that taking the Bitters was the *cause* of my going to sleep. However,
although Doctor Hartshorne's Insomnia Bitters *may* have put
me to sleep, I also may have fallen asleep on my own. Maybe it
had nothing to do with the Bitters. Maybe I was very tired, and
took the Bitters just before I would have fallen asleep anyway.

Doctor Hartshorne could have her day in court. We would
need to set up a controlled experiment, with one group of people
using the Bitters and another group not using it. If more of the
people who used it fell asleep faster than the people who did not
use it, then it may have some medicinal value after all. But mere
correlation, by itself, does not *establish* a cause-and-effect rela-
tionship. The rise and fall of women's hemlines correlated for
years with the rise and fall of the Dow Jones Industrial Average,
but who thinks that one causes the other? The world is just full
of coincidences.

21.   Correlated events may have a common cause

Some correlations are not relations between cause and effect
but represent two effects of some *other* cause. It is quite possible, for instance, that being well read and being open-minded

are both caused by some third factor: by going to college, for example. Being well read, then, might *not* itself lead to open-mindedness: instead, going to college leads to open-mindedness (maybe by exposing a person to many different points of view) and helps a person become well read as well. You may need to survey your friends again and find out which ones went to college!

> Television is ruining our morals. Shows on television portray violence, callousness, and depravity—and just look around us!

The suggestion here is that "immorality" on television causes "immorality" in real life. It is at least as likely, however, that *both* televised "immorality" *and* real-life "immorality" are caused instead by more basic common causes, such as the breakup of traditional value systems, the absence of constructive pastimes, and so on. Or:

> Over the past twenty years, children have watched more and more television. Over the same period, college admission test scores have steadily declined. Watching television ruins your mind.

The suggestion is that watching television causes lower test scores. It would be useful, for a start, if this argument explained exactly how the alleged cause, watching television, leads to this effect (Rule 18). In any case, other explanations may be at least as good. Maybe something quite different accounts for the drop in test scores—a drop in the quality of the schools, for example—which would suggest that the two correlated trends are not related (Rule 20). Then again, some common cause might have led to *both* watching television *and* lower test scores. Quick—think of two or three possibilities yourself.

22. Either of two correlated events may cause the other

Correlation also does not establish the *direction* of causality. If A is correlated with B, A may cause B—but B also may cause A. The very same correlation that suggests that television is ruining our morals, for example, also could suggest that our morals are ruining television. So, in general, yet another kind of alternative explanation needs to be investigated.

This problem affects even the most advanced studies of correlations. Psychologists might devise a test for open-mindedness and a survey of reading habits, give the tests to a representative sample of the population, and then check to see whether an unusually high proportion of the readers are also open-minded. Suppose a correlation indeed exists. It still does not follow that reading *leads* to open-mindedness. Open-mindedness might lead instead to reading! After all, open-minded people may be more likely to seek out a variety of papers and books in the first place. This is one reason that it is important to explain the connections between cause and effect. If you can fill in plausible connections from A to B but not from B to A, then it seems likely that A leads to B rather than vice versa. If B could lead to A as plausibly as A leads to B, though, then you cannot tell which direction the cause goes—or perhaps it goes both ways.

23. Causes may be complex

It's occasionally argued that pedestrian walkways across streets are more dangerous than unmarked streets, because some crosswalks seem to be associated with a high number of accidents. The suggested explanation is that walkways create in their users a false sense of security, which leads them to take risks and therefore have accidents. Remembering Rule 22, though, we also should consider the possibility that the causal connection runs the other way. Maybe, in a manner of speaking, accidents cause crosswalks. Crosswalks don't just appear arbitrarily, after all: they tend to be put where accidents often have happened. But they may not necessarily eliminate the problem. Dangerous places may become less dangerous, but not suddenly safe.

Moreover, once a crosswalk is installed, still more people are likely to use it. So we might well expect the *number* of people involved in accidents at these locations to increase, rather than decrease, although the accident *rate* should decrease.

Clearly this story is a complex one. A false sense of security might well play some role, especially if the accident rate has not decreased as sharply as we might expect. At the same time we should not forget that crosswalks are usually put precisely at places where accidents tend to happen. Again, causes need not be either/or; sometimes the answer is "both."

Many causal stories are complex. Maybe, again, reading makes you more open-minded, but it is surely also true, as Rule 22 pointed out, that open-mindedness is likely to lead some people to read more. Maybe eating a full breakfast improves your health, but maybe healthy people are also precisely people who are inclined to eat a full breakfast in the first place. Don't overstate your conclusion. Seldom do we fasten onto *the* one and only cause. Causal arguments are important because even finding *a* cause is often useful. Just to know that eating a full breakfast is correlated with better health, and *probably* leads to better health, may be enough reason to eat fuller breakfasts.

VI

Deductive Arguments

Consider this argument.

> If there are no chance factors in chess, then chess is a game of pure skill.
>
> There are no chance factors in chess.
>
> Therefore, chess is a game of pure skill.

Suppose for the moment that the premises of this argument are true. In other words, suppose it's true that *if* there are no chance factors in chess, then chess is a game of pure skill—and suppose there *are* no chance factors in chess. You can therefore conclude with perfect assurance that chess is a game of pure skill. There is no way to admit the truth of these premises and deny the conclusion.

Arguments of this type are called *deductive* arguments. That is, a (properly formed) deductive argument is an argument of such a form that if its premises are true, the conclusion must be true, too. Properly formed deductive arguments are called *valid* arguments.

Deductive arguments differ from the sorts of arguments so far considered, in which even a large number of true premises do not guarantee the truth of the conclusion (though sometimes they may make it very likely). In nondeductive arguments, the conclusion unavoidably goes beyond the premises—that's the very point of arguing by example, authority, and so on—whereas the conclusion of a valid deductive argument only makes explicit what is already contained in the premises.

In real life, of course, we can't always be sure of our premises either, so the conclusions of real-life deductive arguments still have to be taken with a few (sometimes many!) grains of salt. Still, when strong premises can be found, deductive forms are very useful. And even when the premises are uncertain, deductive forms offer an effective way of *organizing* an argument, especially an argumentative essay. This chapter presents six common deductive forms with simple examples, each in a section of its own. Chapters VII–IX return to their use in argumentative essays.

24. Modus Ponens

Using the letters **p** and **q** to stand for sentences, the simplest valid deductive form is

> If [sentence **p**] then [sentence **q**].
> [Sentence **p**].
> Therefore, [sentence **q**].

Or, more briefly:

> If **p** then **q**.
> **p**.
> Therefore, **q**.

This form is called *modus ponens* ("the mode of putting": Put **p**, get **q**). Taking **p** to stand for "There are no chance factors in chess" and **q** to stand for "Chess is a game of pure skill," our introductory example follows modus ponens (check it out).

Often an argument in this form is so obvious it does not need to be stated as an official modus ponens at all.

> Since optimists are more likely to succeed than pessimists, you should be an optimist.

This argument could be written

> If optimists are more likely to succeed than pessimists, then you should be an optimist.
>
> Optimists *are* more likely to succeed than pessimists.
>
> Therefore, you should be an optimist.

But the argument is perfectly clear without putting it in this form. At other times, however, writing out the modus ponens is useful.

> If our galaxy has millions of habitable planets, then it seems likely that life has evolved on more than just this one.
>
> Our galaxy *has* millions of habitable planets.
>
> Therefore, it seems likely that life has evolved on more than just this one.

To develop this argument, you must explain and defend both of its premises, and they require quite different arguments (why?). It is useful to state them clearly and separately from the start.

25. Modus Tollens

A second valid deductive form is *modus tollens* ("the mode of taking": Take **q,** take **p**):

If **p** then **q**.

Not-**q**.

Therefore, not-**p**.

Here "Not-**q**" simply stands for the denial of **q**, that is, for the sentence "It is not true that **q**." Similarly for "not-**p**."

Remember Sherlock Holmes's argument, discussed under Rule 1:

> A dog was kept in the stalls, and yet, though someone had been in and fetched out a horse, the dog had not barked. Obviously the visitor was someone whom the dog knew well. . . .

Holmes's argument is a modus tollens:

> If the visitor was a stranger, then the dog would have barked.
>
> The dog did not bark.
>
> Therefore, the visitor was not a stranger.

To write this argument in symbols, you could use **s** for "The visitor was a stranger" and **b** for "The dog barked."

If **s** then **b**.

Not-**b**.

Therefore, not-**s**.

"Not-**b**" stands for "The dog did not bark," and "not-**s**" stands for "The visitor was not a stranger." As Holmes puts it, the visitor was someone whom the dog knew well.

Astronomer Fred Hoyle wielded an interesting modus tollens. To paraphrase a bit:

> If the universe were infinitely old, no hydrogen would be left in it, because hydrogen is steadily converted into helium throughout the universe, and this conversion is a one-way process. But in fact the universe consists almost entirely of hydrogen. Thus the universe must have had a definite beginning.

To put Hoyle's argument in symbols, use **i** to stand for "The universe is infinitely old" and **h** to stand for "No hydrogen is left in the universe."

If **i** then **h**.

Not-**h**.

Therefore, not-**i**.

"Not-**h**" stands for "It is not true that no hydrogen is left in the universe" (or "The universe does contain hydrogen"); "not-**i**" means "It is not true that the universe is infinitely old." Hoyle went on to rephrase the conclusion. Because the universe is not infinitely old, he says, it must have begun at a definite point.

26. Hypothetical Syllogism

A third valid deductive form is *hypothetical syllogism:*

If **p** then **q**.

If **q** then **r**.

Therefore, if **p** then **r**.

For instance:

> If you study other cultures, then you realize the variety of human customs.
>
> If you realize the variety of human customs, then you question your own customs.
>
> Therefore, if you study other cultures, then you question your own customs.

Using the letters in boldface to stand for the component sentences in this statement, we have:

> If **s** then **r**.
>
> If **r** then **q**.
>
> Therefore, if **s** then **q**.

Hypothetical syllogisms are valid for any number of premises as long as each premise has the form "If **p** then **q**" and the **q** of one premise becomes the **p** of the next. Under Rule 6, for example, we considered an argument with the previous two premises but also a third:

> If you question your own customs, then you become more tolerant.

From this and the other two premises, you can validly conclude "If **s** then **t**" by hypothetical syllogism.

Notice that hypothetical syllogism offers a good model for explaining the connections between cause and effect (Rule 18). The conclusion links a cause and an effect, while the premises explain the stages in between.

27. Disjunctive Syllogism

A fourth valid deductive form is *disjunctive syllogism:*

> **p** or **q**.
> Not-**p**.
> Therefore, **q**.

Consider, for instance, Bertrand Russell's argument discussed under Rule 2:

> Either we hope for progress by improving morals, or we hope for progress by improving intelligence.
>
> We can't hope for progress by improving morals.
>
> Therefore, we must hope for progress by improving intelligence.

Again using the boldface letters as symbols, this argument goes

> **m** or **i**.
> Not-**m**.
> Therefore, **i**.

There is a complication. In English the word "or" can have two different meanings. Usually "**p** or **q**" means that at least one of **p** or **q** is true and possibly both. This is called an "inclusive" sense of the word "or" and is the sense normally assumed in logic. Sometimes, though, we use "or" in an "exclusive" sense, in which "**p** or **q**" means that either **p** or **q** is true but *not* both. "Either they'll come by land or they'll come by sea," for example, suggests that they won't come both ways at once. In that case you might be able to infer that if they come one way then they're *not* coming the other way.

Disjunctive syllogisms are valid regardless of which sense of "or" is used (check it out). But what *else* (if anything) you may be able to infer from a statement like "**p** or **q**"—in particular, whether you can conclude not-**q** if you also know **p**—depends on the meaning of "or" in the specific "**p** or **q**" premise you are considering. Take care!

28. Dilemma

A fifth valid deductive form is the *dilemma:*

> **p** or **q**.
> If **p** then **r**.
> If **q** then **s**.
> Therefore, **r** or **s**.

Rhetorically, a "dilemma" is a choice between two options both of which have bad consequences. Jesus posed a dilemma of this sort to the Pharisees when they publicly challenged his authority:

> He answered them, "I also will ask you a question; now tell me, Was the baptism of John from Heaven or from men?" And they discussed it with one another, saying, "If we say, 'From heaven,' he will say, 'Why did you not believe him?' But if we say, 'From men,' all the people will stone us, for they believe that John was a prophet." (Luke 20: 3–6)

Logically, the Pharisees' dilemma is

> Either we say John's baptism was from **h**eaven or that it was from **m**en.
>
> If we say it was from **h**eaven, we will be **b**lamed for not believing him.
>
> If we say it was from **m**en, we will be **s**toned for insulting the popular belief in him.

Therefore, either we will be blamed for not believing him or
we will be stoned for insulting the popular belief in him.

And in symbols:

> **h** or **m.**
> If **h** then **b.**
> If **m** then **s.**
> Therefore, **b** or **s.**

So the Pharisees, sensibly enough, declined to answer at all—
leaving Jesus free to dodge their questions in turn.

In this case, both consequences are bad, but in other dilemmas the consequences might be good, or simply neutral.

> Either we go to the circus or we go skating.
> If we go to the circus, then we'll have a blast.
> If we go skating, then we'll also have a blast.
> Therefore, we'll have a blast.

Technically, the conclusion is "Either we'll have a blast or we'll
have a blast," but saying it once is quite enough.

29.   Reductio ad absurdum

One traditional deductive strategy deserves special mention
even though, strictly speaking, it is only a version of modus
tollens. This is the *reductio ad absurdum,* that is, a "reduction to
absurdity." Arguments by "reductio" (or "indirect proof," as
they're sometimes called) establish their conclusions by showing that assuming the opposite leads to absurdity: to a contradictory or silly result. Nothing is left to do, the argument
suggests, but to accept the conclusion.

To prove: **p.**

Assume the opposite: Not-**p.**

Argue that from the assumption we'd have to conclude: **q.**

Show that **q** *is false (contradictory, silly, "absurd").*

Conclude: **p** must be true after all.

Remember the argument for the existence of a Creator discussed under Rule 12. Houses have creators, the argument goes, and the world is *like* a house—it too is ordered and beautiful. Thus, the analogy suggests, the world must have a Creator too. Rule 12 quoted David Hume to the effect that the world is not relevantly similar enough to a house for this analogy to succeed. In Part V of his *Dialogues* Hume also suggested a reductio ad absurdum of the analogy. Paraphrased:

Suppose the world has a Creator like a house does. Now, when houses are not perfect, we know who to blame: the carpenters and masons who created them. But the *world* is also not wholly perfect. Therefore, it would seem to follow that the Creator of the world is not perfect either. But you would consider this conclusion absurd. The only way to avoid the absurdity, however, is to reject the supposition that leads to it. Therefore, the world does not have a Creator in the way a house does.

Spelled out in reductio form, the argument is:

To prove: The world does not have a Creator in the way a house does.

Assume the opposite: The world *does* have a Creator in the way a house does.

Argue that from the assumption we'd have to conclude: The Creator is imperfect (because the world is imperfect).

But: God cannot be imperfect.

Conclude: The world does not have a Creator in the way a house does.

Not everyone would find the idea of an imperfect God "absurd," of course, but Hume knew that the Christians with whom he was arguing would not accept it.

30. Deductive arguments in several steps

Many valid deductive arguments are *combinations* of the simple forms introduced in Rules 24–29. Here, for example, is Sherlock Holmes performing a simple deduction for Doctor Watson's edification, meanwhile commenting on the relative roles of observation and deduction. Holmes has casually remarked that Watson has been to a certain post office that morning, and furthermore that he sent off a telegram while there. "Right!" replies Watson, amazed, "Right on both points! But I confess that I don't see how you arrived at it." Holmes replies:

> "It is simplicity itself. . . . Observation tells me that you have a little reddish mold adhering to your instep. Just opposite the Wigmore Street Post Office they have taken up the pavement and thrown up some earth, which lies in such a way that it is difficult to avoid treading in it in entering. The earth is of this peculiar reddish tint which is found, as far as I know, nowhere else in the neighborhood. So much is observation. The rest is deduction."
> [Watson]: "How, then, did you deduce the telegram?"
> [Holmes]: "Why, of course I knew that you had not written a letter, since I sat opposite you all morning. I see also in your open desk there that you have a sheet of stamps and a thick bundle of postcards. What could you go to the Post Office for, then, but to send a wire? Eliminate all the other factors, and the one which remains must be the truth."*

Putting Holmes's deduction into more explicit premises, we might have:

---

* A. Conan Doyle, *The Sign of Four* (Garden City, N.Y.: Doubleday & Co., 1974), pp. 17–18.

1. Watson has a little reddish mold on his boots.
2. If Watson has a little reddish mold on his boots, then he has been to the Wigmore Street Post Office this morning (because there and only there is reddish dirt of that sort thrown up, and in a way difficult to avoid stepping in).
3. If Watson has been to the Wigmore Street Post Office this morning, he either mailed a letter, bought stamps or cards, or sent a wire.
4. If Watson had gone to the post office to mail a letter, he would have written the letter this morning.
5. Watson wrote no letter this morning.
6. If Watson had gone to the post office to buy stamps or cards, he would not already have a drawer full of stamps and cards.
7. Watson already has a drawer full of stamps and cards.
8. Therefore, Watson sent a wire at the Wigmore Street Post Office this morning.

We now need to break the argument down into a series of valid arguments in the simple forms presented in Rules 24–29. We might start with a hypothetical syllogism:

2. If Watson has a little reddish mold on his boots, then he has been to the Wigmore Street Post Office this morning.
3. If Watson has been to the Wigmore Street Post Office this morning, he either mailed a letter, bought stamps or cards, or sent a wire.
A. Therefore, if Watson has a little reddish mold on his boots, he either mailed a letter, bought stamps or cards, or sent a wire at the Wigmore Street Post Office this morning.

(I will use *A, B,* etc. to stand for the conclusions of simple arguments, which then can be used as premises to draw further conclusions.) With A and 1 we can use modus ponens:

A. If Watson has a little reddish mold on his boots, he either mailed a letter, bought stamps or cards, or sent a wire at the Wigmore Street Post Office this morning.
1. Watson has a little reddish mold on his boots.

B. Therefore, Watson either mailed a letter, bought stamps or cards, or sent a wire at the Wigmore Street Post Office this morning.

Two of these three possibilities now can be ruled out, both by modus tollens.

4. If Watson had gone to the post office to mail a letter, he would have written the letter this morning.
5. Watson wrote no letter this morning.
C. Therefore, Watson did not go to the post office to mail a letter.

and:

6. If Watson had gone to the post office to buy stamps or cards, he would not already have a drawer full of stamps and cards.
7. Watson already has a drawer full of stamps and cards.
D. Therefore, Watson did not go to the post office to buy stamps or cards.

Finally, we can put it all together:

B. Watson either mailed a letter, bought stamps or cards, or sent a wire at the Wigmore Street Post Office this morning.
C. Watson did not go to the post office to mail a letter.
D. Watson did not go to the post office to buy stamps or cards.
8. Therefore, Watson sent a wire at the Wigmore Street Post Office this morning.

This last inference is an extended disjunctive syllogism. "Eliminate all the other factors, and the one which remains must be the truth."

VII

Composing an Argumentative Essay

A. Exploring the Issue

We now move from writing short arguments to writing longer ones—from arguments in paragraphs to arguments in essays. An argumentative essay is often an elaboration of a short argument, or a series of short arguments held together by a larger design. But the process of thinking and designing an argumentative essay makes it much different from a short argument.

The next three chapters correspond to the three stages of writing an argumentative essay. Chapter VII is about *Exploring the Issue,* Chapter VIII sets out the *Main Points of the Argumentative Essay,* and Chapter IX is about actually *Writing the Essay.* The rules in these chapters are prefixed by an *A, B,* or *C.*

The Introduction distinguished two main uses of arguments: to *inquire* into the merits of a position and to *defend* a position once your inquiry has borne fruit. The first step is inquiry. Before you can write an argumentative essay, you must explore the issue and think through the various positions for yourself.

AI.   Explore the arguments on all sides of the issue

Some people have proposed a "voucher plan" for elementary
and secondary schools. Under this plan, the tax money that
currently goes to the public school system would be divided
equally among children's parents in the form of "vouchers"
which they could transfer to the school of their choice, including private and parochial schools. The government would regu-
late competing schools to make sure that they all met minimal
standards, but people would be free to choose whatever school
they wished as long as it met those standards.

Suppose you are assigned the voucher plan as a topic for an
argumentative essay. Do *not* begin by dashing off an argument
for the opinion that first occurs to you. You are not being asked
for the opinion that first occurs to you. You are being asked to
arrive at a well-informed opinion that can be defended with
solid arguments. It takes some time.

First, find out what each side considers the strongest arguments for its position. Read articles or talk to people with
different viewpoints.

The strongest argument for the pro-voucher side is probably
"freedom of choice." The voucher plan, it is claimed, would
lead to a much wider range of alternative schools than now
exists, and it would not penalize parents for choosing one of
them over another (as the present system does, since everyone
must pay taxes to support the public schools even if their children do not attend). The main argument *against* vouchers seems
to be that the public schools mirror the real world: we have to
learn to live with and appreciate people who are *not* like us and
with whom we might *not* choose to go to school if we had the
choice. Public schools, it is claimed, make democratic citizens.

As you examine the issue, you will find arguments for and
against these claims. You also will begin to formulate arguments of your own. Assess these arguments using the rules in
Chapters I–VI. Try out different argument forms, make as good

an argument as you can for each side, and then criticize these arguments using these rules.

Consider arguments by analogy. Have we tried anything *like* the voucher system before? Perhaps: Competing colleges and universities, though not paid for by vouchers, seem to offer a variety of good educations, which suggests that a system of competing primary and secondary schools might have similar results. But be sure that this is a relevantly similar example. At present, for example, many colleges and universities are tax supported and, at least in theory, are democratically responsive. Would a system without such public institutions offer good educations to as many people? Would it bring as many diverse people into contact?

Maybe schools under the voucher plan have more relevant similarities to the present parochial and private schools. Here you also need some arguments from examples or from authority. How good are the present private and parochial schools compared to the public school system? Do they produce people who work as well with other people?

Deductive arguments also may be useful. Here is a hypothetical syllogism:

> If we set up a voucher plan, then schools would be competing for students.
>
> If schools are competing for students, then they will use advertisements and promotions to encourage parents to "shop around."
>
> If parents are encouraged to "shop around," then many parents will move their children from school to school.
>
> If many parents move their children from school to school, many children will not form lasting friendships or feel secure about their surroundings.
>
> Therefore, if we set up a voucher plan, many children will not form lasting friendships or feel secure about their surroundings.

As Rule 26 pointed out, hypothetical syllogisms often can be used in this way to explain the connections between causes and

effects. They also may be used to *work out* what those connections might be in cases where you are not sure whether there *is* a
connection.

A2.   Question and defend each argument's premises

When the premises of an argument are open to question, you
must consider arguments for *them* as well.

Suppose you are considering the hypothetical syllogism just
sketched. You know that it is a valid argument; the conclusion
does indeed follow from the premises. But you still need to be
convinced that the premises are *true*. To continue exploring the
issue, then, you must go another step: You must try to come up
with arguments for any of the premises of the argument that
reasonably might be questioned.

An argument for the second premise ("If schools are competing for students, then they will use advertisements and promo-
tions to encourage parents to 'shop around'") might use an
analogy:

> When stores compete for customers, they try to offer special
> deals and services to make themselves look more attractive than
> the competition, and they advertise heavily to draw new cus-
> tomers in and old customers back. Then the other stores respond
> with their special deals and advertisements. Customers are drawn
> from store to store and then back again; they believe they can get
> the best deal by shopping around. It would be just the same with
> competing schools. Each school would advertise and offer spe-
> cial deals, and the other schools would respond. Parents would
> shop around just like grocery shoppers or department store cus-
> tomers do now.

Not every claim needs much defense. The first premise of the
hypothetical syllogism ("If we set up a voucher plan, then
schools will be competing for children") is obvious enough to
assert without much argument: this is the whole *idea* of the

voucher plan. The second premise did need an argument, however, and so would the fourth ("If many parents move their children from school to school, many children will not form lasting friendships or feel secure about their surroundings"). You might also have to defend some of the premises of *those* arguments in turn. In the argument for the second premise just suggested, you might go on to offer examples to show that stores do indeed offer special deals and advertise heavily in the face of heavy competition.

Any claim liable to reasonable question needs at least some defense. Naturally, space often will limit what you can say. Given limited space or time, argue chiefly for your most important and most controversial claims. Even then, however, cite at least *some* evidence or authority for any other claims that remain debatable.

A3. Revise and rethink arguments as they emerge

Rules A1 and A2 outline a *process*. You may have to try several different conclusions—even opposite conclusions—before you find a view that can be defended with strong arguments. Even after you have settled on the conclusion you want to defend, you may have to try several forms of argument before you find one that really works. Quite probably your initial argument will have to be improved. Many of the rules in Chapters I–VI illustrate how short arguments must be improved and expanded: by adding examples to an argument by example (Rule 8), by citing and explaining the qualifications of an authority (Rules 13 and 14), and so on. Sometimes you will not be able to find enough examples, so you may have to change your approach (or change your mind!). Sometimes you may go in search of an authority to support a claim you want to make, only to find that most authorities take the opposite view (you probably have to change your mind) or that the most informed people still disagree sharply with one another (and then you cannot argue from authority at all; remember Rule 16).

Take your time—and give yourself time to take. This is a stage where revision is easy and experiments are cheap. You can change your mind without embarrassment, and indeed may have to. For some writers it is the most satisfying and creative part of writing. Use it well!

VIII

Composing an Argumentative Essay

B. Main Points of the Essay

Suppose you have arrived at a conclusion that you think you can defend adequately. Now you need to *organize* your essay so that it covers everything that needs to be covered and so that you can present your argument most effectively. Get out a large sheet of scratch paper and a pencil; you are about to prepare your outline.

B1. *Explain the question*

Begin by stating the question you are answering. Then explain it. Why is it important? What depends on the answer? If you are making a proposal for future actions or policies, like the voucher plan, begin by showing that we presently have a *problem*. Why should others share your worries or be interested in your ideas for change? What led *you* to be concerned?

Consider your audience. If you are writing for a newspaper or public presentation, your audience may be unaware of the issue or unaware of the extent of the problem. Your job is to make them aware. Restating the problem can be useful even when it is no news. It helps to locate your proposal—what problem are you trying to solve?—and it may help remind those who are aware of the problem but who may not have considered its importance. If you are writing an academic essay, however, do not try to restate the whole history of the issue. Find out how much background your instructor expects.

To justify your concern with a particular question or issue, you may need to appeal to shared values and standards. Sometimes these standards are simple and uncontroversial. If you have a proposal about traffic safety, you probably will find that its goals are obvious and uncontroversial. Nobody likes traffic accidents. Other arguments can appeal to standards shared by a specific group, such as professional codes of ethics, or to institutional standards, such as the standards of student conduct a school endorses. They can appeal to the U.S. Constitution and to shared political ideals, like freedom and fairness. They can appeal to shared ethical values, such as the sanctity of life and the importance of individual autonomy and growth, and to broad social values such as beauty and intellectual curiosity.

B2. Make a definite claim or proposal

If you are making a proposal, be specific. "Something should be done" is not a real proposal. You need not be elaborate. "Everyone should eat breakfast" is a specific proposal but also a simple one. However, if you want to argue that the United States should institute a voucher plan, some elaboration is necessary to explain the basic idea, how payments would work, and so on. Similarly, if you are making a philosophical claim, or defending your interpretation of a text or event, first state your claim or interpretation *simply* ("God exists"; "The American Civil War was caused primarily by economic conflicts"; and so on). Elaborate later as necessary.

If your aim is simply to assess some of the arguments for or against a claim or proposal, you may not be making a proposal of your own or even arriving at a specific decision. For example, you may be able to examine only one line of argument in a controversy. If so, make it clear immediately that this is what you are doing. Sometimes your conclusion may be simply that the arguments for or against some position or proposal are inconclusive. Fine! But make that conclusion clear immediately. Begin by saying, "In this essay I will argue that the arguments for X are inconclusive." Otherwise, *your* essay will seem inconclusive!

B3.   *Develop your arguments fully*

Once you are clear about the importance of the issue you are addressing and once you have decided exactly what you intend to do in your paper, you are ready to develop your main argument.

Planning is important. Your paper has limits: Don't fence more land than you can plow. One argument well developed is better than three only sketched. Do *not* use every argument you can think of for your position—this is like preferring ten very leaky buckets to one well-sealed one. (Also, the different arguments may not always be compatible!) Concentrate on your one or two best.

If you are making a proposal, you need to show that it will solve the problem you began with. Sometimes just stating the proposal is enough. If the problem is that your health is suffering because you do not eat a full breakfast, then eating a full breakfast is the obvious solution. If your proposal is that the United States set up a voucher plan, however, then some careful argument is necessary. You need to show that a voucher system really would encourage freedom of choice, that a variety of schools would be available, and that these schools would be a clear improvement over the present schools. You have to argue about cause and effect, argue from example, and so forth, and the rules discussed in previous chapters apply. Use the arguments you began to develop in Chapter VII.

If you are arguing for a philosophical claim, this is the place to develop your main reason(s). If you are arguing for your interpretation of a text or event, this is the place to explain the details of that text or event and to work out your interpretation in detail. If your essay is an assessment of some of the arguments in a controversy, explain those arguments and the reasons for your assessment. Once again, remember the rules from previous chapters. If you rest a claim on an argument by example, be sure you have enough examples, representative examples, and so on. If you use a deductive form, make sure that it is valid and that you defend any questionable premises as well.

B4.   Consider objections

Anticipate skeptical questions. Is your proposal affordable? Will it take too long? Has it been tried before? Can you get people to carry it out? If your proposal will be a difficult one to carry out, admit it; argue that it is worth carrying out all the same.

Most proposals have many effects, not just one. You need to consider what *dis*advantages your proposal might have. Anticipate disadvantages others might raise as objections; bring them up yourself and respond to them. Argue that the advantages outweigh the disadvantages (and be sure, once you've considered them, that they really do!). True, the voucher plan might make schools less stable, but that might seem a small price to pay to make schools more responsive to the wishes of parents and communities. You also can argue that some possible disadvantages will not actually materialize. Maybe the schools will *not* become unstable. After all (use an argument by analogy), businesses are not destabilized when they are forced to respond to changing customer preferences.

Anticipate objections to your claim or interpretation. If you are writing an academic paper, look for criticisms of your claim or interpretation in the class readings. Once you have explored the issue carefully, you also will find objections by talking to people with different views and in your background reading.

Sift through these objections, pick the strongest and most common ones, and try to answer them.

B5.   Consider alternatives

This is an obvious rule but it is constantly overlooked. If you are defending a proposal, it is not enough to show that your proposal will solve a problem. You also must show that it is *better* than other plausible ways of solving that problem under the circumstances.

> The city of Charlotte's swimming pools are overcrowded, especially on weekends. Therefore, Charlotte should expand its pools!

This argument is weak in several ways. "Overcrowded" is vague, and so is the proposal. But remedying these weaknesses will not justify the conclusion. Other and more reasonable ways of ending the crowding may be possible. Maybe the pools should have more open-swim hours so that the crowds can spread themselves over more available times. Maybe the typically light-use times should be more widely publicized. Maybe the pools' hours can be extended (people can swim at night!). Maybe swim teams and other closed-pool activities should be moved off the weekends. Or maybe Charlotte should do nothing at all and let users readjust their usage for themselves. If you still want to argue that Charlotte should build more pools, you must show that your proposal is better than any of these (much less expensive) alternatives.

Similarly, if you are interpreting a text or event, you need to consider alternative interpretations. No matter how cleverly and thoroughly you may explain why something happened, some other explanation may seem more likely. You need to show that other explanations are *less* likely; remember Rule 19. Even philosophical claims have alternatives. Does the argument from creation (under Rule 12) show that *God* exists, for instance, or only that a *Creator* exists who might not necessarily be everything we think of when we speak of "God"? Argument is hard work!

IX

Composing an Argumentative Essay

C. Writing

You have explored your issue and worked out an outline. You are finally ready to write the essay itself. Remember again that writing the formal version is only the *last* stage! If you have just picked up this book and opened it to this chapter, reflect: there is a reason that this is the last chapter and not the first. As the proverbial old Irishman said when a tourist asked him how to get to Dublin, If you want to get to Dublin, don't start here.

Remember too that the rules of Chapters I–VI apply to writing an essay as well as to writing short arguments. Review the rules in Chapter I in particular. Be concrete and concise; avoid loaded language; and so forth. What follow are some additional rules specific to writing argumentative essays.

C1. *Follow your outline*

The previous chapter advised you to get out a large sheet of scratch paper and work out an outline of your argumentative essay. Explain the question, make a definite claim, and so on. Now follow your outline as you begin to write. Don't wander from one point to a related point that is supposed to come later.

If you find as you write that the essay fits together awkwardly, stop and revise your outline; then follow the new one.

C2. Keep the introduction brief

Some students use the entire first page of a four-page argumentative essay simply to introduce the paper, often in general and irrelevant ways.

NO:

> Philosophers for centuries have debated about the existence of God . . .

This is padding. It's no news to anybody. Get right to the point.

YES:

> In this essay I will argue that God exists.

or

> This paper will argue that instituting a voucher system for primary and secondary education would lead to a society of greater intolerance and isolation between people of different classes.

C3. Give your arguments one at a time

As a general rule, make one point per paragraph. Including several different points in the same paragraph only confuses the reader and lets important points slip by.

Use your main argument to plan your paragraphs. Suppose you intend to argue against the voucher system on the grounds that under a voucher system children would not form lasting friendships or feel secure about their surroundings. First, make your intentions clear (Rule B2). Then you might use the hypothetical syllogism already sketched:

> If we set up a voucher plan, then schools would be competing for students.
>
> If schools are competing for students, then they will use advertisements and promotions to encourage parents to "shop around."
>
> If parents are encouraged to "shop around," then many parents will move their children from school to school.
>
> If many parents move their children from school to school, many children will not form lasting friendships or feel secure about their surroundings.
>
> Therefore, if we set up a voucher plan, many children will not form lasting friendships or feel secure about their surroundings.

State this argument first in a paragraph beginning "My main argument will be that . . ." You might not want to include all the steps, but give the reader a clear idea of where you are going. Then, to explain and defend this argument, devote one paragraph to each premise. The first paragraph might be brief, as the first premise does not require much defense; just explain that this is the idea of the voucher plan. The second paragraph might be the short argument for the second premise suggested under Rule A2.

Follow this pattern for all arguments, not just deductions. Recall this argument from Rule 8:

> Women's rights to vote were won only after a struggle.
>
> Women's rights to attend colleges and universities were won only after a struggle.
>
> Women's rights to equal employment opportunity are being won only after a struggle.
>
> Therefore, all women's rights are won only after a struggle.

Once again, a good essay will first explain the importance of the issue, then make the conclusion plain, and then devote a paragraph (sometimes several paragraphs) to each premise. In this argument, a paragraph should defend the first premise by explaining how women won the right to vote, another several paragraphs should defend the second premise by showing with examples what a struggle it was for women to begin attending colleges and universities, and so on.

Notice, in both of these arguments, the importance of using consistent terms (Rule 6). When clearly connected premises such as these become the lead sentences in separate paragraphs, their parallel phrasing holds the whole essay together.

C4. Clarify, clarify, clarify

Maybe you know exactly what you mean; everything is clear to you. Often it is far from clear to anyone else. Points that seem connected to you may seem completely unrelated to someone reading your essay. Thus it is essential to explain the connections between your ideas, even if they seem perfectly clear to you. *How* do your premises relate to each other and support your conclusion?

NO:

> Having a choice of many schools is better than having just one. This is a traditional American value. Thus, we should set up a voucher system.

What is the connection between having many schools and "a traditional American value"? At first glance, in fact, the writer's claim seems to be false. Traditionally, America has favored the single public school. More carefully explained, however, there is an important idea here.

YES:

> Having a choice of many schools is better than having just one. Americans always have valued having choices. We want to have a choice between different cars or foods, between different candidates for office, and between different churches. The voucher system only extends this principle to schools. Thus, we should set up a voucher system.

Clarity is important for yourself as well as for your readers. Points that *seem* connected to you may not *really* be connected, and by trying to make the connections clear you will discover that what seemed so clear to you is not really clear at all. Many times I have seen students hand in an essay they think is sharp and clear, only to find when they get it back that they can barely understand what they themselves were thinking when they wrote it! (Their grades probably aren't too encouraging either.) One good test of clarity is to put your first draft aside for a day or two and then read it again. What seemed clear late Monday night may not make much sense Thursday morning. Another good test is to give your essay to a friend to read. Encourage him or her to be critical!

You also may have to explain your use of certain key terms. You may need to give common terms a meaning more precise than usual for purposes of your essay. This is fine as long as you *explain* your new definition and (of course) stick to it.

C5. *Support objections with arguments*

Naturally, you want to develop your own arguments carefully and fully, but you also need to develop possible arguments on the *other* sides carefully and in detail, if not quite as fully as your own. Suppose, for example, you are defending a voucher plan. When you turn to objections (Rule B4) and alternatives (B5), consider how people would argue against your plan.

NO:

>   Someone might object that the voucher system is unfair to low-income people or children with disabilities. But *I* think that . . .

Why would someone object that the voucher system is unfair? What *arguments* (reasons, not just conclusions) are you responding to?

YES:

   Someone might object that the voucher system is unfair to low-income people or children with disabilities. Children with disabilities may require more school resources than children without disabilities, for instance, but under a voucher system their parents would receive only the same voucher as everyone else. Parents might not be able to make up the difference, and the children would be poorly provided for.

   The objection about low-income families, as I understand it, is this: Low-income families might be able to send their children only to low-budget schools that didn't charge anything above and beyond the voucher, while the rich could afford better and more varied schools. Therefore, it might be objected that the voucher system represents "freedom of choice" only for the rich.

   I would respond to these objections as follows. . . .

Now it is clear exactly what the objections are, and you can try to respond to them effectively. You might, for instance, propose special vouchers for students with disabilities. You might not even have thought of this possibility if you had not detailed the arguments behind the objection, however, and your readers certainly would not have understood the point of special vouchers even if you had mentioned them.

C6.   Don't claim more than you have shown

End without prejudice.

NO:

   In conclusion, every reason seems to favor the voucher plan, and none of the objections stands up at all. Obviously, the United States should adopt a voucher plan as quickly as possible.

YES:

   I have argued in this essay that the United States has at least one good reason to adopt the voucher plan. Although people have raised some serious objections, it seems possible to modify the voucher system to deal with them. It's worth a try.

Maybe the second version overdoes it in the other direction, but you see the point. Very seldom will you answer all the objections adequately, and even when you do, new problems may surface tomorrow. "It's worth a try" is the best attitude.

X

Fallacies

Fallacies are misleading arguments. Many of them are so tempting, and therefore so common, they even have their own names. This may make them seem like a separate and new topic. Actually, however, to call something a fallacy is usually only another way of saying that it violates one of the rules for *good* arguments. The fallacy of "false cause," for example, is simply a questionable conclusion about cause and effect, and you can look to Chapter V for explanation.

To understand fallacies, then, you need to understand what rules they break. This chapter begins by explaining two very general fallacies, referring them back to some of the rules in this book. Following that is a short list and explanation of a number of specific fallacies, including their Latin names when frequently used.

The Two Great Fallacies

One of our most common temptations is to draw conclusions from too little evidence. For example, if the first Lithuanian I meet has a fiery temper, I might jump to the conclusion that *all*

Lithuanians have fiery tempers. If one ship disappears in the Bermuda Triangle, the *National Enquirer* proclaims the Bermuda Triangle haunted. This is the fallacy of *generalizing from incomplete information.*

Consider how many of the rules in Chapters II–VI are directed against this fallacy. Rule 8 requires more than one example: You cannot draw a conclusion about the entire student body of your college based on yourself or your roommate. Rule 9 requires representative examples: You cannot draw a conclusion about the entire student body of your college based on your student friends, even if you have a lot of them. Rule 10 requires background information: If you draw a conclusion about the student body of your college based on a sample of 30 people, you also must consider how big the student body is (30? 30,000?). Arguments from authority require that the *authority* not overgeneralize: He or she must have the information and the qualifications to justify the judgment you quote. Rule 19 warns us not to assume that just because we've found one possible cause for an event, we've therefore found *the* cause. Other causes may still be more likely.

A second common fallacy is *overlooking alternatives.* Rules 20–23 pointed out that just because events A and B are correlated, it does not follow that A causes B. B could cause A; something else could cause *both* A and B; A may cause B *and* B may cause A; or A and B might not even be related. These alternative explanations may be overlooked if you accept the first explanation that occurs to you. Don't rush; there are usually many more alternative explanations than you think.

For example, consider one more argument about causes:

> A good way to avoid divorce is to make love frequently, because figures show that spouses who make love frequently seldom seek divorce.

Frequent lovemaking is correlated with staying married, and is therefore supposed to be the *cause* (or *a* cause) of staying married. But staying married also may lead to frequent lovemaking. Or something else (love and attraction!) may cause both frequent lovemaking and staying married. Or each may cause the other. Or possibly making love and staying married are not even related!

We also often overlook alternatives when we make decisions. Two or three options stand out, and we weigh only these. In his famous essay "Existentialism Is a Humanism," philosopher Jean-Paul Sartre tells of a student of his, during the Nazi occupation of France in World War II, who had to choose between making a risky voyage to England to fight with the Free French and staying with his mother in Paris to look after her. Sartre paints the picture as if the young man must either stake everything on a flight to England and thus totally abandon his mother, or else commit himself entirely to her and give up any hope of fighting the Nazis. But surely he had other possibilities. He could have stayed with his mother and still worked for the Free French in Paris; or he could have stayed with his mother for a year and tried to ensure her position, gradually making it possible to leave. And are we to think of his mother as completely dependent and graspingly selfish, or was she perhaps a little patriotic and possibly self-sufficient too? Had he even asked her what she wanted? Very likely, then, the student had other options.

On ethical issues too we tend to overlook alternatives. We say that either the fetus is a human being with all the rights you and I have, or else it is a lump of tissue with no moral significance at all. We say that either every use of animal products is wrong or all of the current uses are acceptable, and so on. Again, however, surely other possibilities exist. Try to increase the number of options you consider, not narrow them!

Some Classical Fallacies

ad hominem: attacking the *person* of an authority rather than his or her qualifications. See Rule 17.

ad ignorantiam (appeal to ignorance):   arguing that a claim is true just because it has not been shown to be false. A classic example is this statement by Senator Joseph McCarthy when he was asked for evidence to back up his accusation that a certain person was a Communist:

> I do not have much information on this except the general statement of the agency that there is nothing in the files to disprove his Communist connections.

ad misericordiam (appeal to pity):   appealing to pity as an argument for special treatment.

> I know I flunked every exam, but if I don't pass this course, I'll have to retake it in summer school. You *have* to let me pass!

Pity is not always a bad argument, but it is certainly inappropriate when objective evaluation is called for.

ad populum: appealing to the emotions of a crowd; also, appealing to a person to go along with the crowd. "Everyone's doing it!" Ad populum is a good example of a *bad* argument from authority: No reasons are offered to show that "everybody" is an informed or impartial source.

affirming the consequent: a deductive fallacy of the form

> If **p** then **q**.
>
> **q**.
>
> Therefore, **p**.

In the statement "if **p** then **q**," **p** is called the "antecedent" and **q** the "consequent." The second premise of a modus ponens—a valid form—affirms (asserts) the antecedent (check it out). Affirming the *consequent,* though, yields an invalid form. A true conclusion is not guaranteed even if the premises are true. For example:

> When the roads are icy, the mail is late.
>
> The mail is late.
>
> Therefore, the roads are icy.

Although the mail *would* be late if the roads were icy, it also may be late for other reasons. This argument overlooks alternative explanations.

begging the question: implicitly using your conclusion as a premise.

> God exists because it says so in the Bible, which I know is true because God wrote it, after all!

To write this argument in premise-and-conclusion form, you'd have to write

> The Bible is true, because God wrote it.
>
> The Bible says that God exists.
>
> Therefore, God exists.

To defend the claim that the Bible is true, the arguer claims that God wrote it. But, obviously, if God wrote the Bible, God exists. Thus the argument *assumes* just what it is trying to prove.

circular argument: same as **begging the question.**

complex question: posing a question or issue in such a way that people cannot agree *or* disagree with you without committing themselves to some other claim you wish to promote. A simple example: "Are you still as self-centered as you used to be?" Answering either "yes" *or* "no" commits you to agreeing that you used to be self-centered. More subtle example: "Will you follow your conscience instead of your pocketbook and donate to the cause?" Saying "no," regardless of their real reasons for not donating, makes people feel guilty; saying "yes," regardless of their real reasons for donating, makes them noble. If you want a donation, the honest thing is just to ask for it.

denying the antecedent: a deductive fallacy of the form

> If **p** then **q**.
> Not-**p**.
> Therefore, not-**q**.

In the statement "If **p** then **q**," **p** is called the "antecedent" and **q** the "consequent." The second premise of a modus tollens—a valid form—denies the consequent (check it out). Denying the *antecedent,* however, yields an invalid form. A true conclusion is not guaranteed even if the premises are true. For example:

> When the roads are icy, the mail is late.
> The roads are not icy.
> Therefore, the mail is not late.

Although the mail *would* be late if the roads were icy, it also may be late for other reasons. This argument overlooks alternative explanations.

equivocation: see Rule 7.

false cause: generic term for a questionable conclusion about cause and effect. To figure out specifically *why* the conclusion is (said to be) questionable, turn to Rules 20–23.

false dilemma: reducing the options you consider to just two, often sharply opposed and unfair to the people the dilemma is posed against. For example, "America: Love it or Leave it." Here is a more subtle example from a student paper: "Since the universe could not have been created out of nothingness, it must have been created by an intelligent life force. . . ." Is creation by an intelligent life force the *only* other possibility? False dilemmas often include **loaded language;** they also, obviously, overlook alternatives.

loaded language: see Rule 5.

non sequitur: drawing a conclusion that "does not follow," that is, a conclusion that is not a reasonable inference from the evidence. Very general term for a bad argument. Try to figure out specifically what is supposed to be wrong with the argument.

the "person who" fallacy: see Rule 10.

persuasive definition: defining a term in a way that appears to be straightforward but that in fact is **loaded.** For example, Ambrose Bierce, in *The Devil's Dictionary,* defines "faith" as "belief without evidence in what is told by one who speaks without knowledge, of things without parallel." Persuasive definitions may be favorably loaded too: for example, defining "conservative" as "someone with a realistic view of human limits." See the Appendix on definition.

petitio principii: Latin for **begging the question.**

poisoning the well: using **loaded language** to disparage an argument before even mentioning it.

I'm confident you haven't been taken in by those few holdouts who still haven't outgrown the superstition that . . .

More subtle:

> No sensitive person thinks that . . .

post hoc, ergo propter hoc (literally, "after this, therefore because of this"): assuming causation too readily on the basis of mere succession in time. Again a very general term for what Chapter V tries to make precise. Turn to Chapter V and try to figure out specifically *why* the argument is supposed to assume causation too readily.

red herring: introducing an irrelevant or secondary subject and thereby diverting attention from the main subject. Usually the red herring is an issue about which people have strong opinions, so that no one notices how their attention is being diverted. In a discussion of the relative safety of different makes of cars, for instance, the issue of which cars are made in America is a red herring.

straw man: caricaturing an opposing view so that it is easy to refute; see Rule 5.

weasel word: changing the meaning of a word in the middle of your argument so that your conclusion can be maintained, though its meaning may have shifted radically. Usually a maneuver performed under the pressure of a counterexample.

> A.   All studying is torture.
> B.   What about studying argument? You love that!
> A.   Well, that's not really studying.

Here "studying" is the weasel word. A's response to B's objection in effect changes the meaning of "studying" to "studying that is torture." A's first statement remains true, but only at the cost of becoming trivial ("All studying that is torture is torture"). See also the discussion of "selfish" under Rule 7, and the Appendix on definition.

APPENDIX

Definition

Some arguments require attention to the meaning of words. Sometimes we may not know the established meaning of a word, or the established meaning may be specialized. If the conclusion of your argument is that "Wejacks are herbivorous," your first task is to define your terms, unless you are speaking to an Algonquian ecologist.* If you encounter this conclusion elsewhere, the first thing you need is a dictionary.

Other times, a term may be in popular use but still be unclear. We debate "assisted suicide," for example, but don't necessarily understand exactly what it means. Before we can argue effectively about it, we need an agreed-upon idea of what we are arguing *about*.

Still another kind of definition is required when the meaning of a term is contested. What is a "drug," for example? Is alcohol a drug? Is tobacco? What if they are? Can we find any logical way of answering these questions?

---

* "Wejack" is the Algonquian name for the fisher, a weasel-like animal of eastern North America. "Herbivores" are animals that eat only or mostly plants. Actually, wejacks are not herbivorous.

D1.   When terms are unclear, get specific

Start with the dictionary. A neighbor of mine was taken to task
by the city's Historic Districts Commission for putting up a
four-foot model lighthouse in her front yard. City ordinances
prohibit any yard fixtures in historic districts. She was hauled
before the commission and told to remove it. A furor erupted
and it got into the newspapers.

Webster's saved the day. According to the dictionary, a "fixture" is something fixed or attached as to a building, such as a
permanent appendage or structural part. The lighthouse, however, was moveable—more like a lawn ornament. Hence, not a
"fixture"; hence, not prohibited.

When issues get more difficult, dictionaries are less helpful.
Dictionary definitions often offer synonyms, for one thing, that
may be just as unclear as the word you're trying to define.
Dictionaries also may give multiple definitions, so you have to
choose between them. And sometimes dictionaries are just
plain wrong. *Webster's* defines "headache" as "a pain in the
head." This is too broad a definition. A bee sting or cut on your
forehead or nose would be a pain in the head but not a headache.

For some words, then, *you* need to make the term more
precise. Use concrete, definite terms rather than vague ones
(Rule 4). Be specific without narrowing the term too much.

> "Organic foods" are foods produced without chemical fertil-
> izers or pesticides.

Definitions like this call a clear idea to mind, and you can go on
to investigate or evaluate it. Also be sure, of course, to *stick* to
your definition as you go on with your argument (Rule 7; see
also the fallacy of weasel word, Chapter X).

Don't use loaded terms (Rule 5). One virtue of the dictionary
is that it is fairly neutral. *Webster's* defines "abortion," for example, as "the forcible expulsion of the mammalian fetus pre-
maturely." This is an appropriately neutral definition. It is not
up to the dictionary to decide if abortion is moral or immoral.

Compare a common definition from one side of the abortion debate:

"Abortion" means "murdering babies."

This definition is loaded. Fetuses are not the same as babies, and the term "murder" unfairly imputes evil intentions to well-intentioned people (however wrong the writer may think they are). That ending the life of a fetus is comparable to ending the life of a baby is an arguable proposition, but it is for an argument to *show,* not simply *assume* by definition. (See also the fallacy of "persuasive definition," Chapter X.)

You may need to do a little research. You will find, for example, that "assisted suicide" means allowing doctors to help aware and rational people arrange and carry out their own dying. It does not include allowing doctors to "unplug" people without their consent (that would be some form of "involuntary euthanasia"—another category). People may have good reasons to object to assisted suicide so defined, but if the definition is made clear at the outset, at least the contending parties will be talking about the same thing.

Sometimes we can define a term by specifying certain tests or procedures that determine whether or not it applies. This is called an *operational* definition. For example, Wisconsin law requires that all legislative meetings be open to the public. But what exactly counts as a "meeting" for purposes of this law? The law offers an elegant operational test:

A "meeting" is any gathering of enough legislators to block action on the legislative measure that is the subject of the gathering.

This definition is far too narrow to define the ordinary word "meeting." But it does accomplish the purpose of this law: to prevent legislators from making crucial decisions out of the public eye.

D2.   When terms are contested, work from the clear cases

Sometimes a term is *contested*. That is, people are arguing over the proper application of the term itself. In that case, it's not enough simply to propose a clarification. A more involved kind of argument is needed.

When a term is contested, you can distinguish three relevant sets of things. One set includes those things to which the term clearly applies. Second are those things to which the term clearly does *not* apply. In the middle will be those things whose status is unclear—including the things being argued over. Your job is to formulate a definition that

1. *Includes* all the things that the term clearly fits;
2. *Excludes* all the things that the term clearly does not fit; and
3. Draws the *plainest possible line* somewhere in between, and *explains* why the line belongs there and not somewhere else.

For example, consider what defines a "bird." Exactly what *is* a bird, anyway? Is a bat a bird?

To meet requirement 1, it is often helpful to begin with the general category (*genus*) to which the things being defined belong. For birds, the natural genus would be animals. To meet requirements 2 and 3, we then need to specify how birds differ from other animals (this is called the *differentia*). Our question therefore is: Precisely what differentiates birds—*all* birds and *only* birds—from other animals?

It's trickier than it may seem. We can't draw the line at flight, for example, because ostriches and penguins don't fly (so the proposed definition wouldn't cover all birds, violating the first requirement) and bumblebees and mosquitoes do (so the proposed definition would include some nonbirds, violating the second).

What distinguishes all and only birds, it turns out, is having feathers. Penguins and ostriches have feathers even though they don't fly—they're still birds. But insects do not, and neither (in case you were wondering) do bats.

Now consider a harder case: What defines a "drug"?

Start again with the clear cases. Heroin, cocaine, and marijuana are clearly drugs. Air, water, most foods, and shampoos are clearly *not* drugs—though all of these are "substances," like drugs, and are all ingested or applied to our body parts. Unclear cases include tobacco and alcohol.*

Our question, then, is: Does any general description cover *all* of the clear cases of "drugs" and *none* of the substances that clearly aren't drugs, drawing a clear line in between?

A "drug" has been defined—even by a presidential commission—as a substance that affects mind or body in some way. But this definition is far too broad. It includes air, water, food, and so on, too, so it fails on the second requirement.

We also can't define a "drug" as an *illegal* substance that affects mind or body in some way. This definition might cover more or less the right set of substances, but it does not meet requirement 3. It does not explain why the line belongs where it is. After all, part of the point of trying to define "drug" in the first place might well be to decide which substances *should* be legal and which should not! Defining a "drug" as an illegal substance short-circuits this project.

Try this:

> A drug is a substance used primarily to alter the state of the mind in some specific way.

Heroin, cocaine, and marijuana obviously count. Food, air, and water don't—because even though they have effects on the mind, the effects are not specific, and are not the primary reason

---

* Unclear in another way are substances such as aspirin, antibiotics, vitamins, and antidepressants—the kinds of substances we buy in "drugstores" and call "drugs" in a pharmaceutical sense. But these are *medicines*—not "drugs" in the moral sense we are exploring.

why we eat, breathe, and drink. Unclear cases we then approach with the question, Is the *primary* effect *specific* and on the *mind?* Perception-distorting and mood-altering effects do seem to be what we are concerned about in current moral debates about "drugs," so arguably this definition captures the kind of distinction people really want to make.

Should we add that drugs are addictive? Maybe not. Some substances are addictive but not drugs—certain foods, perhaps. And what if a substance that "alters the state of the mind in some specific way" turns out to be *non*addictive (as some people have claimed about marijuana, for example)? Is it therefore not a drug? Maybe addiction defines "drug *abuse,*" but not "drug" as such.

D3.   Don't expect definitions to do the work of arguments

Definitions help us to organize our thoughts, to group like things with like, and to pick out key similarities and differences. Sometimes, after words are clearly defined, people may even discover that they do not really disagree about an issue at all. By themselves, though, definitions seldom settle difficult questions.

We seek to define "drug," for example, partly to decide what sort of stance to take toward certain substances. But such a definition cannot answer this question by itself. On the proposed definition, for example, coffee is a drug. Caffeine certainly alters the state of the mind in specific ways. It is even addictive. But does it follow that coffee should be banned? No—because the effect is mild and socially positive for many people. Some attempt to weigh benefits against harms is necessary before we can draw any conclusions.

Marijuana is a drug under the proposed definition. Should *it* (continue to) be banned? Just as with coffee, more argument is necessary. Some people claim that marijuana has only mild and socially positive effects too. Supposing they're right, you could argue that marijuana shouldn't be banned even though it *is* a "drug" (like, remember, coffee). Others argue that it has far worse effects and tends to be a "gateway" to harder drugs besides. If they're right, you could argue for banning marijuana whether it is a drug or not.

Or perhaps marijuana is most akin to certain antidepressants and stimulants—medicines that (take note) turn out to be "drugs" on the proposed definition too, but call not for bans but for *control*.

Alcohol, meanwhile, *is* a drug on the proposed definition. In fact, it is the most widely used drug of all. Its harms are enormous, including kidney disease, birth defects, half of all traffic deaths, and more. Should it be limited or banned? Maybe—though there are counterarguments too. Once again, though, this question is not settled by the determination that alcohol is a drug. Here the *effects* make the difference.

In short, definitions contribute to clarity, but seldom do they make arguments all by themselves. Clarify your terms—know exactly what questions you're asking—but don't expect that clarity alone will answer them.

Next Steps

The subject of this book is usually labeled "critical thinking" or (less commonly now) "informal logic." If you're a high school or college student and want to learn more about the subject, look for courses with these titles being offered in your school. If you want to read more, you can find dozens of textbooks for such courses in any college or university library under keywords such as "critical thinking." Two good representative examples are *Critical Thinking,* by Brooke Noel Moore and Richard Parker (Mayfield Publishing Company) and *Open Minds and Everyday Reasoning,* by Zachary Seech (Wadsworth Publishing Company).

The study of formal logic begins with the deductive forms presented in Chapter VI and expands them into a symbolic system of much greater scope and power. A good representative textbook is *A Concise Introduction to Logic,* by Patrick Hurley (Wadsworth Publishing Company)—but again there are dozens available (search under "logic"). Many textbooks now combine both formal and informal logic. A balanced overview of both is *The Art of Reasoning,* by David Kelley (W. W. Norton).

On the role of critical thinking in ethics, as well as for

some advice about how to avoid overlooking alternatives, see my book *A 21st Century Ethical Toolbox* (Oxford University Press). For more on the "how to" of creative thinking—how to come up with genuinely new alternatives in seemingly "stuck" situations—see the many works of Edward DeBono, such as *DeBono's Thinking Course* (Ariel/BBC).

The field of *rhetoric* studies the persuasive use of language, especially in arguments. One excellent text in the field is *The Aims of Argument: A Rhetoric and Reader,* by Timothy Crusins and Carolyn Channell (Mayfield Publishing Company). A literary approach to argumentation from this angle is *The Realm of Rhetoric,* by Chaim Perelman (University of Notre Dame Press).

Specifically on the fallacies (Chapter X), see Howard Kahane's *Logic and Contemporary Rhetoric* (Wadsworth Publishing Company). For historical and theoretical treatment of the fallacies, see *Fallacies,* by C. Hamblin (Methuen). For citation styles, a useful short guidebook is *Writing with Sources,* by Gordon Harvey (Hackett Publishing Company). On style in general, still unmatched is William Strunk and E. B. White's *The Elements of Style* (Macmillan)—a book in spirit much like this one. Keep them together on a shelf somewhere, and don't let them gather dust!